Shakespeare's
INSULTS

Shakespeare's INSULTS

EDUCATING YOUR WIT

**WAYNE F. HILL
AND CYNTHIA J. ÖTTCHEN**

THREE RIVERS PRESS • NEW YORK

Published by Three Rivers Press, New York, New York.
Member of the Crown Publishing Group.

Random House, Inc. New York, Toronto, London, Sydney, Auckland
www.randomhouse.com

Originally published by Main Sail Press.
First Crown Trade Paperback edition published in 1995.

THREE RIVERS PRESS is a registered trademark and the Three Rivers
Press colophon is a trademark of Random House, Inc.

Printed in the United States of America

Library of Congress Cataloging-in-Publication Data
Shakespeare, William.
Shakespeare's insults / [compiled by] Wayne F. Hill, Cynthia J. Öttchen.
1. Shakespeare, William—quotations.   2. Invective—quotations,
maxims, etc.   3. Quotations, English.   I. Hill, Wayne F.   II. Öttchen,
Cynthia J.   III. Title.
PR2892.H55   1995   822.2'3—dc20   95-30760

ISBN 0-517-88539-5

15 14

Look, he's winding up the watch of his wit; by and by it will strike.

—WILLIAM SHAKESPEARE
The Tempest

CONTENTS

HOW TO HANDLE THIS BOOK

PEOPLE *need* insults. Most people behave so abominably that they cry out for abuse. Charity moves us to meet this need. Abuse is a form of attention, and a little accommodating attention makes anyone feel human again.

But in this backhanded humanity the mere shouting of common profanities will never suffice. Nor, by themselves, will your purple gestures. Fill your lungs, certainly, and figo your fingers, but as The Complete Person you must advance that agile turn of phrase, that chosen word, that little touch of Shakespeare in the night.

Shakespeare gets the last word. He marshals the robust humility that doesn't mind admitting human indignity. Indeed, he points out frailties with subtlety and power. He can lend you just the fulsome, dripping line to drop on your pretentious boss, your mother-in-law, that other driver. The most celebrated pen in the world's most widely spoken language exults in barbs. Indulge yourself. His genius sticks. This book collects the smartest stings ever to snap from the tip of an English-speaking tongue. Go practice. Begin in the mirror.

You can use this book in a hundred ways. Keep it near at hand. By the telephone. On your desk. In your pocket. Have an insult ready at the back of your mind. A few favorite slurs, discovered in Shakespeare, become your own once you've slung them several times. Add a few more for variety, and your day-to-day diction becomes magnificent. Just when you need it to be.

Flip off innuendoes one at a time. Speak plain cannon, fire and smoke and bounce. Or make a more glorious gesture: send the whole book, starred and circled and turned down at the corners for best effect, to that whoreson caterpillar, that base contagion that treads upon your patience.

All of Shakespeare's great insults are here served up. A trestle table heaped with succulent ridicule, dished out in endless variety. Some have been pulled, roots, leaves and all, out of their contexts, only to show fresh colour on the plate. The speakers are left unmentioned to give the words full range. Some crackling bits have acquired nuances unimagined by Shakespeare himself: he launched them on the world, and they have made their own fortunes. Gathered here from all the Bard's plays are juicy morsels with which you can bait the hollow bosoms of fools and asses, gilded butterflies and foul bunch-backed toads.

This book comes to you in three parts. The first is a mass of short, sharp, quick and ready-to-use vituperation. The astonishing variety offers so many vivid examples that you can begin to see how Shakespeare fashioned his insults. We've tried to make his methods apparent by whistling up a mob of knaves and villains just to show how each one of these scurrilous characters is an individual in his own right. People deserve special treatment. But if direct insults do not suit your temperament, we have also supplied an outburst of Shakespearean expletives so you can mutter convincingly under your breath.

The second part carries you play by play where you'll savour the round and full mastery of Shakespeare's wit. He understands the human heart and knows what behavior to expect. The characters he invents, in the circumstances he foresees, give rise to his finest and funniest insults.

The third section of the book is an index of topical scorn. You can equip yourself in advance to meet any situation and every sort of character. Ask yourself what aggravates you above all else. By preparing to confront what annoys you most, you avoid that common regret: the gleaming retort thought of too late.

      Shakespeare's insults are a treasure. Choose a richly coloured stone to throw, and, in genuine generosity, make your nemesis feel like somebody.

Wayne Frederick Hill
Cynthia J. Öttchen

Michaelmas 1991
Queens' College, Cambridge

Thanks to Dr. James Carleton Paget, Walter Herriot and St. John's Innovation Centre, Frederick and Martha Hill, Irmgard Möller, Walter Oettchen, Rob Reti, and Lorna Sargeant for helping to speed Shakespeare's Insults on their way.

We also thank the president and fellows of Queens' College for permission to reproduce the Martin Droeshout portrait from the third folio.

And not least we acknowledge the good humour of the Queens' College porters.

PART I

NAME-CALLING

SPEAK, *breathe, discuss, brief, short, quick, snap! Be ready when the need arises. It's vain to re-live lost opportunities for saying what must be said. Avoid self-recrimination. Spare yourself the wit of the staircase. This array of Shakespearean invective can prepare you to lay out large meaning in little time. The tip of your tongue shows the back of your mind.*

These short insults are ready to use. Practice these thousand raw tricks and by sheer exposure learn to play upon the words. When you do indeed exhale what Shakespeare inspires, your large humility and verbal magnificence may relax the tensions created by knots of prating coxcombs and vile braggarts. The very freshness of your phrases may ventilate the stuffy boors.

We have set out these insults in the singular. If you simply must take on whole riots of fools at once, these slurs work in the plural, too.

GENERAL ABUSE

You drone; snail; slug; sot; ass; drunkard; churl; malt-horse; capon; idiot; patch; minion; baggage; goer-backward; cuckold; drudge; empiric; taffeta punk;

[19]   scolding queen; scurvy lord; witty fool; clog; timorous thief;
rude boy; caitiff; hater of love; despiteful Juno; filthy officer;
jackanape with scarves; ring-carrier; hilding; bubble; hourly
promise-breaker; notable coward; infinite and endless liar;
coxcomb; sprat.

[38]   Counterfeit module;
double-meaning prophesier; past-saving slave; botcher's
'prentice; shrieve's fool; dumb innocent; foolish idle boy;
dangerous and lascivious boy; damnable both-sides rogue;
flinty Tartar; snipt-taffeta fellow; unbaked and doughy
youth; red-tailed bumble-bee; carbonadoed face; hideous
object; common gamester; perfidious slave; equivocal companion; common customer; wrangling queen; common liar;
saucy eunuch; amorous surfeiter; monstrous malefactor;
strange serpent; ribaudred nag; you kite; Jack; boggler; old
ruffian; triple-turn'd whore; witch; vile-lady; old dog; mechanic slave; odd worm; whoreson devil; mortal wretch;
venomous fool; unworthy brother; peasant; envious emula-
tor; monster; nature's natural; cutter-off of nature's wit;
cur; mannish coward; clownish fool; toad.

[87]   Fat and greasy citizen; roynish clown; dog-ape;
compact of jars; you of basest function; cock; rude despiser
of good manners; natural philosopher; crooked-pated old
cuckoldy ram; nut; dull fool; saucy lackey; fancy-monger;
mannish youth; foul slut; confirmer of false reckonings;
puisny tilter; noble goose; common executioner; nature's
sale-work; abominable fellow; tyrant; motley-minded gentleman; ill-favored virgin; idle creature; saucy fellow; common laugher; eternal devil; fleering tell-tale; serpent's egg;
old feeble carrion; shrewd contriver; carcass fit for hounds;
barren-spirited fellow; jigging fool; monstrous apparition;
peevish schoolboy; disguised cheater.

[125]   Prating mountebank; cuck-
old-mad; horn-mad; prating peasant; unfeeling fool; foolish
gnat; hind; curtal dog; drunken slave; backfriend; shoulder-

clapper; Lapland sorcerer; devil; devil's dam; fiend; doting [136] wizard; dissembling harlot; peevish officer; unhappy strumpet; mere anatomy; mountebank; threadbare juggler; fortuneteller; fat friend; belly; rascal; dissentious rogue; quartered slave; fragment; shame of Rome; base slave; fusty plebeian; debile wretch; hereditary hangman; old crab-tree; horse-drench; kitchen malkin; vengeance proud; time-pleaser; flatterer; foe to nobleness; Triton of the minnows; old goat; rotten thing; viperous traitor; general lout; common cry of curs; bastard; daw; dastard noble; carbonado; decayed dotant; varlet; foreign recreant; boy of tears.

Measureless liar; false hound; basest thing; beggar; vile one; that-way-accomplished courtier; [180] flattering rascal; depender on a thing that leans; runagate; saucy stranger; whoreson jackanapes; whoreson dog; Jack-slave; banished rascal; crafty devil; unpaved eunuch; base wretch; base slave; profane fellow; precious pander; precious varlet; injurious thief; rustic mountaineer; empty purse; clotpoll; irregulous devil; sad wrack; kitchen trull; unspeaking sot; most credulous fool; egregious murderer; dullard; implorator of unholy suits; adulterate beast; garbage; wretch whose natural gifts were poor; pernicious woman; addicted so and so; fishmonger; satirical rogue; tedious old fool.

You quintessence of dust; rogue and peasant [221] slave; dull and muddy-mottled rascal; pigeon-liver; whore; guilty creature; breeder of sinners; robustious, periwig-pated fellow; groundling; passion's slave; galled jade; croaking raven; peacock; bosom black as death; wretched, rash, intruding fool; mildewed ear; king of shreds and patches; tardy son; sweet wag; Diana's forester; minion of the moon; Monsieur Remorse; Sir John Sack and Sugar; madcap; thou latter spring; all-hallown summer; true-bred coward; fat rogue; slovenly unhandsome corse; popinjay;   forgetful man; thorn; canker; sword-and-buckler prince; wasp-stung

[256] and impatient fool; vile politician; king of smiles; fawning greyhound; cozener; man of falsehood; foot land-raker; long-staff sixpenny striker; mad mustachio purple-hued maltworm; false thief; fat-kidneyed rascal; veriest varlet that ever chewed with a tooth; whoreson caterpillar; fat chuff; arrant coward; shallow, cowardly hind; lack-brain; frosty-spirited rogue; pagan rascal; infidel; mad-headed ape; paraquito; loggerhead; leathern-jerkin, crystal-button, knot-pated, agate-ring, puke-stocking, caddis-garter, smooth-tongue, Spanish-pouch.

[279]   You damned brawn; shotten herring; woolsack; son of darkness; clay-brained guts; knotty-pated fool; whoreson obscene greasy tallow-catch; pintpot; ticklebrain; naughty varlet; ungracious boy; tun of man; trunk of humours; bolting hutch of beastliness; swoll'n parcel of dropsies; huge bombard of sack; stuffed cloakbag of guts; roasted Manningtree ox with the pudding in his belly; that reverend Vice; that grey Iniquity; father Ruffian; Vanity in years; old white-bearded Satan; Whoremaster; natural coward without instinct; velvet guard; Sunday citizen; smiling pickthanks; base newsmonger; shallow jester; rash bavin wit; capering fool; younker; whoreson, impudent, embossed rascal; nimble-footed madcap; soused gurnet; revolted tapster.

[316]   Canker of a calm world and a long peace; tattered prodigal; scarecrow; mad wag; poor unminded outlaw sneaking home; chewet; fickle changeling; poor discontent; rag-of-muffin; hot termagent; blunt monster with uncounted heads; hulk; hilding fellow; dullest peasant in the camp; foolish compounded clay-man; whoreson mandrake; whoreson Achitophel; whoreson smooth-pate; hunt counter; ill angel; beastly feeder; common dog; bastardly rogue; honeyseed rogue; man-queller and woman-queller; hempseed; scullion; rampallian; fustilarian; poor mad soul; offending Adam; base tike; Iceland dog; prick-eared cur of Iceland; egregious dog;

braggart vile; damned furious wight; hound of Crete; lazar   [351]
kite of Cressid's kind; cunning fiend; poor miserable wretch;
devil incarnate; vain, giddy, shallow, humorous youth;
coward dog; cullion; swasher; white-livered and red-faced;
prince of fiends; bastard warrior; most lofty runaway; arrant
counterfeit rascal; bawd; cutpurse; gull; wretched and
peevish fellow; foolish cur.

Valiant flea; foul and ugly witch; bad neigh-   [372]
bour; prating coxcomb; wretched slave with a body filled and
vacant mind; child of hell; superfluous lackey; hilding foe;
island carrion; damned and luxurious mountain-goat; roaring devil; base pander; Jack-sauce; fellow of no merits; base
Troyan; mountain-squire; squire of low degree; cutpurse of
quick hand; fellow of infinite tongue; prater; effeminate
prince; dastard foeman; Jack-out-of-office; lean raw-boned
rascal; hare-brained slave; distrustful recreant.

Dunghill groom; peeled   [398]
priest; usurping proditer, manifest conspirator; tawny coat;
scarlet hypocrite; foe to citizens; wretched sinner; woeful
man; high-minded strumpet; noisome stench; poor servitor;
fiend of hell; deceitful dam; partaker of a little gain; improvi-
dent soldier; trull; silly dwarf; weak and writhled shrimp;
bloodthirsty lord; riddling merchant; pernicious usurer;
viperous worm; shameless courtesan; hag of all despite;
base muleter; peasant footboy; miscreant;   hedge-born
swain; presumptuous vassal; traitorous rout; ireful bastard; giglet wench; upstart; fell banning hag; decrepit miser;
base ignoble wretch; graceless, cursed drab; presumptuous
dame; base and humble mind; tedious stumbling-block;
contemptuous base-born callet; image of pride; false fiend;
sicked spirit; meanest groom; foul offender.

Idle rascal; hindmost man; bedlam brainsick duch-   [445]
ess; fraudful man; crafty murderer; uncivil kern; mean-born
man; starved snake; shag-haired crafty kern;   basilisk;

[455] hollow friend; loathsome leper; contumelious spirit; arrogant controller; blunt-witted lord ignoble in demeanor; stern untutored churl; false murd'rous coward.

[462]   Pernicious bloodsucker of sleeping men; fell serpent; rude unpolished hind; busy meddling fiend; obscure and lowly swain; jaded groom; base slave; hag of hell; paltry, servile, abject drudge; lowly vassal; vile benzonian; banditto slave; silken-coated slave; false caterpillars; thou serge, thou buckram lord; rude companion; burly-boned clown; audacious traitor; fell-lurking cur; heap of wrath; foul indigested lump; mad misleader; foul stigmatic; sturdy rebel; false peer; poltroon; timorous wretch; brat; she-wolf; Amazonian trull; proud insulting boy; butcher; crook-back; foul misshapen stigmatic; shameless callet; wrangling woman; homely swain; fearful-flying hare; fatal screech-owl.

[501]   You chaos; unlick'd bear-whelp; murderous Machiavel; half malcontent; feigned friend; bug; quicksand of deceit; scolding crookback; wilful boy; untutor'd lad; misshapen Dick; bloody cannibal; devil's butcher; peevish fool; indigest deformed lump; sour annoy; butcher's cur; malicious censurer; ravenous fish; sick interpreter; weak one; giant traitor; devil-monk; bold bad man; living murmurer; most malicious foe.

[527]   Dilatory sloth; hollow heart; false professor; stubborn spirit; most arch heretic; poor undeserver; proud traitor; thou scarlet sin; piece of scarlet; rank weed; lousy footboy; rude slave; fire-drake; wife of small wit; calf; cow; half-face; Sir Knob; sparrow; insolent cracker; thou unadvised scold; cank'red grandam; scroyle; jade; purpose-changer; sly divel; daily break-vow; smooth-fac'd gentleman; all-changing word; false blood; ramping fool; cold-blooded slave; recreant limb; meddling priest; arch-heretic; most sweet lout; thou odiferous stench;

carrion monster; uncleanly scruples; foolish rheum; lean [564] unwash'd artificer; dunghill; beardless boy; cock'red silken wanton; misbegotten divel; clod; vassal; idle old man; whoreson man; clotpoll; mongrel; base football player; degenerate bastard; marble-hearted fiend; detested kite; eater of broken meats; lily-livered, action-taking, whoreson, glass-gazing, super-serviceable, finical rogue; one-trunk-inheriting slave; brazen-faced varlet.

Whoreson cullionly barbermonger; [586] ancient ruffian; whoreson zed; thou unnecessary letter; wagtail; reverent braggart; embossed carbuncle; unnatural hag; the foul fiend Flibbertigibbet; she-fox; ingrateful fox; filthy traitor; milk-livered man; moral fool; vain fool; dog-hearted daughter; thou side-piercing sight; simp'ring dame; rascal beadle; scurvy politician; gilded butterfly; most toad-spotted traitor; low-spirited swain; base minnow of mirth; unlettered small-knowing soul; transgressing slave; most acute juvenal; old love-monger; wimpled, whining, pur-blind, wayward boy; senior-junior, giant-dwarf, Dan-Cupid; regent of love-rhymes; lord of folded arms; anointed sovereign of sighs and groans; liege of all loiterers and malcon-tents; dread prince of plackets.

King of codpieces; [621] sole imperator and great general of trotting 'paritors; perni-cious and indubitate beggar; most simple clown; foolish extravagant spirit; most profane coxcomb; whoreson loggerhead; turtle; barren practiser; half-penny purse of wit; pigeon-egg of discretion; mouse; figure pedantical; some carry-tale; some please-man; some slight zany; some mum-ble-news; some trencher's knight; some Dick, that smiles his cheek in years; libbard's head; pure wit; foolish mild man; cittern-head; Fortune's closestool; head of a bodkin; death's face in a ring; man replete with mocks; rebel's whore; rump-fed ronyon; rat without a tail; imperfect speaker; instrument of darkness; spongey officer; infirm of purpose;

[655]   Porter of Hell Gate; you equivocator; you common enemy of man; you half a soul; water-rug; demi-wolf; best o' th' cut-throats; grown serpent; horrible shadow; unreal mock'ry; magot-pie; close contriver of all harms; secret, black, and midnight hag; filthy hag; you egg; young fry of treachery; infected mind; cream-fac'd loon; lily-liver'd boy; patch; whey-face; liar, and slave; clamorous harbinger of blood and death; Hell-bound; juggling fiend; coward; cruel minister; sanctimonious pirate; Madam Mitigation; tapster; parcel-bawd; tedious fool; wicked varlet; caitiff; wicked Hannibal; death's fool; you poor worm; outward-sainted deputy; beast; faithless coward; dishonest wretch; wicked bawd; whoremaster; whoremonger; bawd-born; motion generative.

[701]   You very superficial, ignorant, unweighing fellow; ungenitured agent; notorious bawd; unlawful bawd; gravel heart; rude wretch; rotten medlar; virgin-violator; wicked'st caitiff on the ground; arch-villain; pernicious caitiff; blasting and scandalous breath; saucy friar; very scurvy fellow; unreverend and unhallow'd friar; goodman baldpate; fleshmonger; thou damnable fellow; giglet; bald-pated, living rascal; punk; want-wit; Sir Oracle; fool gudgeon; death's head with a bone in his mouth; dumb-show.

[727]   Sponge; fawning publican; evil soul; goodly apple rotten at the heart; cut-throat dog; very devil incarnate; younker; prodigal; carrion Death; gossip Report; bankrupt; wanton gambol; soft and dull-eyed fool; most impenetrable cur; bragging Jack; lewd interpreter; wit-snapper; stony adversary; inhuman wretch; brassy bosom; rough heart of flint; inexecrable dog.

[749]   You louse; cony-catching rascal; you Banbury cheese; thou mountain foreigner; latten bilbo; bully-rook; bully Hercules; base Hungarian wight; tinder-box; varlet vile; Mars of malcontents; larron; scurvy Jack-a-nape priest;

greasy knight; drawling, affecting rogue; secure fool; gibbet; thou unconfinable baseness; cuckoldy rogue; mechanical salt-butter rogue; damned Epicurean rascal; Lucifer; Wittol; Cuckold; secure ass; King-Urinal; Monsieur Mock-water; scurvy Jack-dog priest. [762]

Scall, scurvy, cogging companion; you little Jack-a-Lent; unwholesome humidity; gross watery pumpion; lisping hawthorn-bud; dissembling knight; dishonest rascal; foolish carrion; turd; mountain of mummy; panderly rascal; brazen-face; old, cozening queen; you baggage; you polecat; you ronyon; poor unvirtuous fat knight; superstitious idle-headed eld; boor; thick-skin; muscle-shell; vile worm; hodge-pudding; bag of flax; puffed man; old, cold, withered, and of intolerable entrails; great lubberly boy; spotted and inconstant man; jaws of darkness; waggish boy; thou lob of spirits; fat and bean-fed horse; rash wanton; progeny of evils; you hard-hearted adamant; spotted snake with double tongue. [777]

Thorny hedgehog; lack-love; kill-courtesy; hempen homespun; cowardly, giantlike ox-beef; shallowest thickskin of that barren sort; thou cat; thou burr; vile thing; you juggler; you canker blossom; you thief of love; you counterfeit; you puppet; thou painted maypole; vixen; you dwarf; you minimus, of hind'ring knotgrass made; you bead; you acorn; king of shadows; you runaway; idle gaud; patched fool; dear Lady Disdain; hard heart; rare parrot-teacher; hypocrite; professed tyrant; flouting Jack; obstinate heretic; young start-up; old cuckold with horns on his head. [813]

Piece of valiant dust; clod of wayward marl; Prince's jester; toothpicker; my Lady Tongue; double heart; mother of fools; contaminated stale; ill singer; foul blot; vane blown with all winds; block; wild heart; little hangman; truant; hobby-horse; scab; true drunkard; deformed thief; vile thief; [846]

[866] One Deformed; illegitimate construction; approved wanton; common stale; most foul; thou pure impiety; foul-tainted flesh; strange sore; Count Comfect; thou naughty varlet; candle-waster; thou dissembler; dotard; braggart; Jack; milksop.

[882]   Scambling, outfacing, fashion-mongering boy; Calf's head; capon; woodcock; Lord Lackbeard; cursing hypocrite; shallow fool; wronger; offender; quondam carpet-monger; Don Worm; slanderous tongue; double-dealer; martyr slain in Cupid's wars; Signior Sooth; Pilch; Patch-breech; craver; rudeliest welcome to this world.

[901]   Poor inch of nature; roastmeat for worms; gosling; young foolish sapling; malkin; harpy; lown; peevish baggage; herb woman; thou damned door-keeper; coistrel; baboon; basest groom; fairy motion; sad fool; ancient substitute; weak slave; heartless hind; transparent heretic; man of wax; wanton light of heart; candle-holder; small, grey-coated gnat; round little worm; princox; loathed enemy; dull earth; open-arse; poperin pear; young waverer; pale hard-hearted wench; Prince of Cats; courageous captain of compliments; fashion-monger; saucy merchant; flirt-gill; skains-mate; you rat-catcher; Good King of Cats; braggart; worm's meat; wretched boy; sober-suited matron; serpent heart; beautiful tyrant; fiend angelical; dove-feather'd raven; wolvish-ravening lamb; despised substance of divinest show.

[950]   Mistress minion you; you green-sickness carrion; you tallow-face; young baggage; disobedient wretch; mumbling fool; wretched puling fool; whining mammet; dishclout; most wicked fiend; caitiff wretch; thou detestable maw; thou tomb of death; fiend of hell; rotten apple; aglet-baby; old trot; woodcock; irksome bawling scold; wildcat; thou hilding of a devilish spirit; rascal fiddler; twanging Jack; craven; mad-cap ruffian;

swearing Jack; greybeard; wrangling pedant; a very toad;   [975]
preposterous ass; old pantaloon; pedascule; mad-brain
rudesby; frantic fool; jolly surly groom; tired jade; mad
master; you three-inch fool; you logger-headed and unpolish'd
groom; you peasant swain.

You whoreson malt-horse drudge; heedless jolthead;   [990]
unmanner'd slave; proud disdainful haggard; thou false
deluding slave; thou thread; thou thimble; thou flea; thou
nit; thou winter-cricket thou; thou rag; thou quantity; thou
remnant; crack-hemp; mad ass; foul contending rebel;
counter-caster; thou foul thief; thou silly gentleman; finder
out of occasions; night-brawler; lewd minx; young and
sweating devil; simple bawd; subtle whore; thou weed; thou
public commoner; impudent strumpet; insinuating rogue;
cogging, cozening slave; scurvy fellow; young quat; notable
strumpet; trash; perjured woman; dolt; murderous coxcomb;
puny whipster; demi-devil; Spartan dog; false trembling
coward; recreant and most degenerate traitor; overwheening
traitor.

You gilded loam; you painted clay;   [1033]
out-dared dastard; caitiff recreant; traitor, foul and dangerous; guilty soul; lunatic, lean-witted fool; most degenerate;
a parasite; keeper-back of Death; banished traitor; caterpillar of the commonwealth; thou coward majesty.

Thou little better thing than earth; nimble mis-   [1046]
chance; dishonorable boy; you Pilate; thou haught, insulting man; thou ladder; unruly woman; unthrifty son; young
wanton and effeminate boy; commonest creature; treacherous son; shrill-voiced supplicant; sour husband; frantic
woman; hardhearted lord; jealous o'erworn widow; nighty
gossip; creeping venomed thing; black magician;
unmannered dog; thou dreadful minister of hell; thou lump
of foul deformity; diffused infection of a man; devilish slave;
hedgehog; rancorous enemy; silken, insinuating Jack; thou

[1074] cacodemon; wrangling pirate; foul wrinkled witch; peevish brat; thou hateful withered hag; troubler of the world's peace; thou elvish-marked, abortive, rooting hog; slave of nature and the son of hell; thou slander of thy heavy mother's womb; thou loathed issue of thy father's loins; thou rag of honour; bottled spider; poisonous bunch-backed toad; malapert; lunatic; simple gull; sour ferryman; foul fiend; erroneous vassal; traitor to the name of God; incapable and shallow innocent.

[1094] You idle weed; parlous boy; covert'st sheltered traitor; tongueless block; iron-witted fool; unrespective boy; little peevish boy; hellhound; foul defacer of God's handiwork; excellent grand tyrant of the earth; carnal cur; Hell's black intelligencer; petty rebel; relenting fool; shallow, changing woman; doubtful, hollow-hearted friend; white-livered runagate; wretched, bloody, and usurping boar; foul swine; tardy sluggard; you base foul stone falsely set; paltry fellow; milksop; overwheening rag; famished beggar; poor rat; heir of shame; perfect gallows; you bawling, blasphemous, incharitable dog; whoreson, insolent noise-maker; wide-chapp'd rascal; enemy inveterate; malignant thing; damn'd witch; blue-eyed hag; freckled whelp hag-born; dull thing; you slave, who never yields us kind answer; thou earth, thou; thou tortoise; poisonous slave; thou most lying slave, whom stripes may move, not kindness; filth as thou art; abhorred slave; thing most brutish; you hag-seed; beauty's canker.

[1141] Spendthrift of tongue; strange fish; holiday fool; most delicate monster; moon-calf; glass-fac'd flatterer; bawd between fold and want; fool in good clothes; thou damned baseness; thou disease of a friend; sworn rioter; most smiling, smooth, detested parasite; courteous destroyer; affable wolf; meek bear; you fool of fortune; trencher-friend; cap-and-knee slave; you vapour; minute-Jack; curl'd-pate ruffian; carper; cap of all fools alive; thou issue of a mangy

dog; thou tedious rogue; thou bright defiler of Hymen's [1165]
purest bed; poor fragment; slender ort; gross patchery; foul-
spoken coward; pretty brabble; saucy controller of private
steps; unmannerly intruder; foul adultress; fell cur of
bloody kind.

You stony image, cold and dumb; thou map [1176]
of woe; base bondsman; joyless, dismal, black, and sorrow-
ful issue; hellish dog; sanguine, shallow-hearted boy; ye
white-limed wall; ye alehouse painted sign; long-tongued
babbling gossip; sly frantic wretch; incarnate devil; wall-
eyed slave; most insatiate and luxurious woman; inhuman
traitor; ravenous tiger, accursed devil; unhallowed slave;
execrable wretch.

Breeder of dire events; [1193]
sneaking fellow; porridge after meat; chaff and bran;
drayman; thou bitch-wolf's son; thou mongrel beef-witted
lord; toadstool; porpentine; thou loathsomest scab in Greece;
cobloaf; whoreson cur; thou stool for a witch; thou sodden-
witted lord; scurvy-valiant ass; thou thing of no bowels; vile
owl; fusty nut with no kernel; trash; one besotted on sweet
delights; gilt counterfeit; paltry, insolent fellow; great-siz'd
monster of ingratitude; valiant ignorance; puling cuckold;
still and dumb-discoursive devil that tempts most cun-
ningly; theme of all our scorns; thou core of envy; thou
crusty botch of nature; idol of idiot-worshippers; fragment;
thou full dish of fool; thou damnable box of envy; you
ruinous butt; you whoreson indistinguishable cur; thou idle
immaterial skein of sleeve silk; thou green sarsenet flap for
a sore eye; thou tassel of a prodigal's purse.

Thou finch egg; louse of a lazar; [1231]
herring without a roe; puttock; sweet sink; sweet sewer;
incontinent varlet; dissembling abominable varlet; crafty
swearing rascal; stale old mouse-eaten dry cheese; thou
boy-queller; most putified core; thou great-siz'd coward;

[1244] broker-lackey; fellow o' th' strangest mind i' th' world; dry fool; mouse of virtue; thou ordinary fool, that has no more brain than a stone; pickle-herring; thou cruell'st she alive; babbling gossip.

[1252] Thou common recreation; time-pleaser; affectioned ass; rascally sheep-biter; metal of India; fellow of servants, not worthy to touch Fortune's fingers; gross acquaintance; gull-catcher; notable contempt; thou most excellent devil of wit; corruptor of words; dear venom; dear manikin; foul collier; firago; hyperbolical fiend; thou dishonest Satan; notable pirate, thou salt-water thief; uncivil lady; marble-breasted tyrant; you very devil incardinate; you passy mesaures pavin; ass-head; votary to fond desire; worthless post; testy babe; exceeding puppet; sourest-natured dog that lives; you very pebble stone; you kind of chameleon; notable lubber.

[1283] Jolt-head; illiterate loiter; thou subtle, perjured, false, disloyal man; you whoreson peasant; foolish lout; thou counterfeit to thy true friend; thou friend of an ill fashion; thou common friend that's without faith or love; fellow false; cold coward; dainty dominie; you most coarse frieze capacity, ye jean judgment; scornful piece; scurvy hilding; Babion with long tail and eke long tool; scorn of women; changeling; leprous witch; polled bachelor; simp'ring sire; abandoner of revels; mute contemplative; dam of horror; sow of lead; you wanton calf; flax-wench; gross lout; mindless slave; thou thing; bed-swerver; mankind witch; most intelligencing bawd; callat of boundless tongue; gross hag; boil'd brains; snapper-up of unconsidered trifles; low-born lass; queen of curds and cream; stretch-mouthed rascal; thou fresh piece of excellent witchcraft; pedlar's excrement; old sheep-whistling rogue.

[1325] You are a needy, hollow-eyed, sharp-looking wretch; a living dead man; one o' th' false ones; this imperceiverant

thing; a very drudge of nature's; a very drab; such a dish of [1329]
skim milk; an ingrate and cankered; one not worth a
gooseberry; so vile a lout; you are son and heir of a mongrel
bitch; a boil; a plague-sore; a new Gorgon; a mind diseas'd;
a list of an English kersey; one that serves a bad woman; a
breath thou art; an ass-head; a very valiant trencher-man;
a stuffed man; a very forward March-chick; a very dull fool;
merely a dumb-show; one relish'd of a base descent; the very
butcher of a silk button; one half-lunatic; one full of spleen;
a very monster in apparel.

                    Such a snipe; all in all spleen [1354]
and nothing of a man; one light of brain; what a slug; the
sweating lord; a dumb statue or breathing stone; a very
shallow monster; a very weak monster; a most poor credulous monster; a puppy-headed monster; a most perfidious
and drunken monster; a most scurvy monster; a most
ridiculous monster; you are the wonder of a poor drunkard;
a howling monster; one opposite to humanity; one whose
grossness little characters sum up; a very camel; a slave
whose gall coins slanders like a mint; a botchy core; a filthy
piece of work; a very land-fish, languageless; a dog-fox not
proved worth a blackberry; a very filthy rogue; a coward and
a coistrel; a very renegado; a most devout coward, religious
in it; one full of bread and sloth; a most unbounded tyrant;
a mere dull shadow; a mere gypsy.

        You rabble of vile confederates; herd of boils and [1385]
plagues; souls of geese; brace of unmeriting, proud, violent,
testy magistrates (alias fools); tongues o' th' common mouth;
petty spirits of region low; foul and pestilent congregation of
vapors; some quantity of barren spectators; gentlemen of
the shade; base contagious clouds; foul and ugly mists of
vapours; ye fat-guts; such toasts-and-butter; discarded
unjust servingmen; nest of hollow bosoms; men of grosser
blood; sworn brothers in filching; men proud of destruction;
barbarous people; frosty people; slanders of the age; fat-

[1407] brained followers; a sort of naughty persons; a sort of tinkers, rascal people; simple men; giddy people; men of malice; wanton boys that swim on bladders; faithful friends o' th' suburbs; bastards and else; degenerate, bloody Neroes; rude multitude; summer-flies; kernes and gallowglasses; weird women; crew of wretched souls; strangely-visited people; our rarer monsters; wild and wanton herd; geminy of baboons; newts and blind-worms.

[1426] Crew of patches; rude mechanicals, that work for bread; a college of wit-crackers; new tuners of accent; strange flies; these pardon-me's; unconstant womankind; pictures out of doors; devils being offended; rough, rug-headed kernes which live like venom; dogs easily won to fawn on any man; Judases, each one thrice worse than Judas; noisome weeds; so dissolute a crew; kites and buzzards; a knot of damned bloodsuckers; a nest of spicery; a sort of vagabonds, rascals, and runaways; scum of Britains and base lackey peasants.

[1445] The most needless creatures living; usurer's men, you knot of mouth-friends; time's flies; general filths; fools on both sides; crows and daws; thieves unworthy of a thing so stol'n; dull and factious nobles; mutable, rank-scented meiny; vagrom men; troll-my-dames; such water-flies and diminutives of nature; brethren and sisters of the hold-door trade; scoundrels and subtractors; fools' zanies; store of muttons; poor slight sores; some severals of head-piece extraordinary.

KNAVERY AND VILLAINY

Shakespeare can spin gold from ordinary words. Take plain "knaves" and "villains." He attaches qualities to them of one or several kinds. He props comparatives or opposites up against them. He recruits verbs to push and pull

*them. He marks wide borders out around them and makes
them capitals of Christendom or of the whole world.*

Foul-mouthed and caluminous knave, wrangling   [1463]
knave, poor gallant knave, shrewd knave and unhappy;
poor, decayed, ingenius, foolish, rascally knave; foul knave;
knave that smells of sweat; Fortune's knave; fantastical
knave; naughty knave; Sir knave; sly and constant knave;
arrant knave; untaught knaves; bacon-fed knaves; gorbellied
knaves; rascally yea-forsooth knave; a young knave and
begging; arrant, malmsy-nose knave; the rascally, scauld,
beggarly, lousy, pragging knave; scurvy, lousy knave; a
counterfeit cowardly knave; crafty knaves; a subtle knave;
the lying'st knave in Christendom; By holy Mary, there's
knavery! lazy knaves; thou most untoward knave; my lord's
knave; base, proud, shallow, beggarly, three-suited, hun-
dred-pound, filthy worsted-stocking knave; beastly knave;
stubborn ancient knave; muddy knave; unthrifty knave;
jealous rascally knave; poor cuckoldy knave; jealous wittoly
knave; lousy knave; lunatic knave; shrewd and knavish
sprite; a couple of as arrant knaves as any; little better than
false knaves; scurvy knave; what a pestilent knave is this
same; whoreson beetle-headed, flap-ear'd knave; knave
very voluble; a pestilent complete knave; a slipper and
subtle knave; a devilish knave; most villainous knave; base
notorious knave; most unjust knave; scurvy, doting, foolish
knave; scurvy railing knave; a good knave; a thin-faced
knave; beat the knave into a twiggen-bottle.

Horrible villain; villain of the earth;   [1516]
soulless villain; secret and villainous contriver; trusty vil-
lain; whoreson senseless villain; dissembling villain; hungry, lean-faced villain; insolent villain; all-worthy villain;
thou villain base; thou double villain; geck and scorn o' th'
other's villainy; smiling, damned villain; bloody, bawdy
villain; remorseless, treacherous, lecherous, kindless villain; stoney-hearted villains; villainous abominable misleader

[1534] of youth; honeysuckle villain; a craven and a villain; base dunghill villain and mechanical; abhorred villain, unnatural, detested, brutish villain; abominable villain; strange and fasted villain; unbolted villain; resolved villain; thou shag-hair'd villain; thou bloodier villain than terms can give thee out; precise villains; villain with a smiling cheek; plain-dealing villain; rich villain; villainy which did confirm any slander; liberal villain; bastards whose spirits toil in frame of villainies; one approved in the height a villain; God should go before such villains! villain that is hither come in spite; villain that fights by the book of arithmetic; condemned villain; senseless villain; whoreson villain; you notorious villain; closet lock and key of villainous secrets; eternal villain; villainous whore; notorious villain; fleshed villains; dull unmindful villain; villain boy; a very excellent piece of villainy; detestable villain; barbarous, beastly villain like thyself; whoremasterly villain; branded villain; chaffy lord not worth the name of villain; villain fit to lie unburied.

EXPLETIVES

Sudden eruptions vent overwrought passions. These pungent outbursts take form as interjections, exclamations, expletives. Even muttered under your breath at no one in particular, they sound like insults. They carry the force of immediate response to the press of human folly.

[1572]   God's mercy! God shield! A pox on't! O strange men! Foh! Fie! Fie on thee! Leprosy o'ertake! O this false soul! Thou spell! O rarely base! Cupid have mercy! Woe the while! What rubbish and what offal! O piteous spectacle! O woeful day! 'Sdeath! O' my word! O' my troth! Pluto and hell! To th' pot! For the love of Juno! Pow-waw! Plague upon't! Breath of garlic-eaters! Puttock! Puppies! O, vengeance, vengeance!

O, all the devils! O most delicate fiend! Fie on't, ah, Fie! O day [1600] and night! Chops! Come away and be hanged! God's body! A plague on thee! A plague of sighing and grief! A pox on this gout! or a gout on this pox! The Lord lighten thee! 'Twould drink the cup and all!

P̲ish! Pish for thee! O viper [1612] vile! Go to! By my troth! Let floods o'erswell, and fiends for food howl on! By Cheshu! By Chrish, la! So Chrish save me! Die and be damned! Figo for thy friendship! The fig of Spain! The figo for thee then! O diable! The devil take order now! A plaguing mischief light on thee! Tush! O miserable age! O monstrous! O gross and miserable ignorance! Ah, barbarous villains! Shame and confusion! O unbid spite! The devil fiddle 'em! Plague of your policy! Body o' me! By holy Mary! Mercy o' me! Out on thee! Bedlam, have done! Zounds! Bad world the while! By Jupiter! Heaven and earth! Fut! Darkness and devils! Blasts and fogs upon thee! My breath and blood! Vengeance, plague, death, confusion! Fie, foh, and fum! O my little heart! A pox of that jest!

O̲ poverty in wit! O Hell-kite! By my troth! Go mend, [1654] go mend! How now! Go to kennel! A pox o' your throats! Fie upon him! Injurious world! How much low peasantry! O, these deliberate fools! Goodly Lord! Tut a pin! Good worts! The tevel and his tan! Froth and scum! By cock and pie! Peace your tattlings! Hue and cry! O cross! O spite! O hell! By'r Lakin! God shield us! O strange! By Jesu! Switch and spurs! Out upon you! By my heel! Zounds! The plague o' both your houses! God's bread! Ancient damnation! Cock's passion! O immortal gods! O heaven! O treason of the blood! O villainous! A fig! O heavy ignorance! Blessed fig's end! Blessed pudding! Pish! Zounds, that's fulsome! Piss o' th' nettle! Divinity of hell! O wretched fool! O curse of marriage! Death and damnation! O, blood, blood, blood! By yond marble heaven! Goats and monkeys! Fire and brimstone! Alas! Hell gnaw his bones! Ud's pity! Beshrew me! O heavens

[1709]   forfend! O heavenly Powers! Go to, charm your tongue! O ill-dispersing wind of misery! Despiteful tidings! The red plague rid you! Warm o' my troth! Mercy, mercy! Traffic confound thee, if the gods will not! Hang thyself! Hoy-day! The gods fall upon you! Hang thee, monster!

[1723]   A pox of wrinkles! Consumption catch thee! The plague of company light upon thee! Vengeance rot you all! O gods, how do you plague me! Chaff and bran! Porridge after meat! Crows and daws! Fie for godly shame! A pestilence on you! Go hang yourself! A bugbear take you! Hey-day! Sprites and fires! O plague and madness! O wither'd truth! A burning devil take you! Misprision in the highest degree! A plague o' these pickle-herring! Tilly-vally! Go shake your ears! Bolts and shackles! Fire and brimstone! Hang him, plum porridge! Disgrace and blows! Let all the dukes and all the devils roar! God's lid! Go rot! Good sooth!

PART II

THE PLAYS

SHAKESPEARE *tunes his insults to the spirit of the play.* Much Ado About Nothing *runs lightly. The play spurs us to keep up with Beatrice's sarcasm. Indeed, Benedick fairly speaks for all of us, who need quick ears, when he wishes his horse had the speed of her tongue.* Coriolanus, *by contrast, spits acerbity.*

> *They lie deadly that tell you have good faces.*

Timon of Athens *stands close to* Coriolanus, *pronouncing bitter misanthropy and resenting his expense of breath and the waste of the stones he throws. He would beat all men, but it would infect his hands.*

The history plays plumb the descending order of the world. King Henry V loftily proclaims the waste of God's supreme creation in the traitor's second fall of man. Great nobles throw down courtly challenges. Lesser figures vent in earthier terms: thou dunghill! Comical characters scathe themselves in their abuses of the language, throwing lines beyond the useful range of invective.

And that brings us once again to the practical usefulness of this book. Let Shakespeare stand beside you so you don't write yourself down an ass but goad those other braying ass-heads into public light.

We define insults broadly. Some sit smug at the center of the definition, clearly intended to cast aspersion. Others come from around the edges—like disparaging insinuations, self-judgements or cynical observations. Shakespeare uses them all to put every sort of character in his just place.

Shakespeare is meant to be performed. Like theater directors, therefore, we have taken some decisions for theatrical force. We've done such obvious things as replace the archaic 'and' with 'if,' and 'a' with 'he.' Oddities we've kept are marked with 'sic.' We've dropped in bracketed pronouns, [like this], in place of proper names. Rather than say 'Richard is' we have said '[you are]' to create direct address. Thus we've jolted familiar quotations to newly awakened uses. This unearths disparagement that is indeed present, but sometimes lends it unexpected meaning. We've also dispensed with ellision marks when resurrecting these dismembered insults from the damp and clinging matter of the plays.

All's Well That Ends Well

Is there no military policy how virgins might blow up   [1752]
men?

                                        1. 1. 119-20

[Your] virginity breeds mites, much like a cheese.   [1753]

                                        1. 1. 139

Your date is better in your pie and your porridge than in   [1754]
your cheek.

                                        1. 1. 154-55

Your virginity, your old virginity, is like one of our French   [1755]
wither'd pears: it looks ill, it eats drily.

                                        1. 1. 156-57

If I can remember thee I will think of thee at court.   [1756]

                                        1. 1. 184-85

You go so much backward when you fight.   [1757]

                                        1. 1. 196

Get thee a good husband, and use him as he uses thee.   [1758]

                                        1. 1. 210-11

[1759] [Their] judgments are
Mere fathers of their garments.

1. 2. 61-62

[1760] [Their] constancies
Expire before their fashions.

1. 2. 62-63

[1761] The complaints I have heard of you I do not all believe;
'tis my slowness that I do not; for I know you lack not
folly to commit them and have ability enough to make
such knaveries yours.

1. 3. 8-11

[1762] If I be his cuckold, he's my drudge.

1. 3. 43-44

[1763] We might have a good woman born before every blazing
star or at an earthquake.

1. 3. 83-84

[1764] Thus he his special nothing ever prologues.

2. 1. 91

[1765] [You show yourself] highly fed and lowly taught.

2. 2. 3

[1766] [This] is like a barber's chair that fits all buttocks: the
pin-buttock, the quatch-buttock, the brawn-buttock, or
any buttock.

2. 2. 16-18

[1767] You would answer very well to a whipping.

2. 2. 50-51

[1768] 'Tis strange, 'tis very strange; that is the brief and the tedious of it.

2. 3. 28-29

He's of a most facinerious spirit.   [1769]

2. 3. 29-30

If thou be'st not an ass, I am a youth of fourteen.   [1770]

2. 3. 100-1

I will throw thee from my care for ever   [1771]
Into the staggers and the careless lapse
Of youth and ignorance.

2. 3. 162-64

The scarfs and the bannerets about thee did manifoldly   [1772]
dissuade me from believing thee a vessel of too great a
burden.

2. 3. 202-4

So, my good window of lattice, fare thee well; thy case-   [1773]
ment I need not open, for I look through thee.

2. 3. 213 14

My lord, you give me most egregious indignity.   [1774]
Ay, with all my heart; and thou art worthy of it.

2. 3. 215-16

You do me most insupportable vexation.   [1775]

2. 3. 227

Scurvy, old, filthy, scurvy lord!   [1776]

2. 3. 232

Thou wert best set thy lower part where thy nose stands.   [1777]

2. 3. 247-48

[1778] If I were but two hours younger I'd beat thee.

2. 3. 249-50

[1779] Methink'st thou art a general offence and every man should beat thee.

2. 3. 250-51

[1780] I think thou wast created for men to breathe themselves upon thee.

2. 3. 251-52

[1781] You are a vagabond and no true traveller.

2. 3. 255-56

[1782] You are not worth another word, else I'd call you knave.

2. 3. 258-59

[1783] France is a dog-hole.

2. 3. 270

[1784] So that you had her wrinkles and I her money.

2. 4. 19

[1785] To say nothing, to do nothing, to know nothing, and to have nothing, is to be a great part of your title, which is within a very little of nothing.

2. 4. 23-26

[1786] Much fool may you find in you, even to the world's pleasure and the increase of laughter.

2. 4. 34-35

[1787] One that lies three thirds and uses a known truth to pass a thousand nothings with, should be once heard and thrice beaten.

2. 5. 28-30

There can be no kernel in this light nut; the soul of this [1788]
man is his clothes.

2. 5. 42-44

Here comes my clog. [1789]

2. 5. 53

The brains of my Cupid's knock'd out, and I begin to love [1790]
as an old man loves money, with no stomach.

3. 2. 14-16

Till I have no wife I have nothing. [1791]

3. 2. 74

[He is] a very tainted fellow, and full of wickedness. [1792]

3. 2. 87

You did never lack advice so much [1793]
As letting her pass so.

3. 4. 19-20

She is too mean to have her name repeated. [1794]

3. 5. 60-61

Were I his lady [1795]
I would poison that vile rascal.

3. 5. 83-84

[You] jackanapes with scarves! [1796]

3. 5. 85

He's a most notable coward, an infinite and endless liar, [1797]
an hourly promise-breaker, the owner of no one good
quality.

3. 6. 9-11

When his disguise and he is parted tell me what a sprat [1798] you shall find him.

3. 6. 100-1

[1799]   I spoke with her but once
And found her wondrous cold.

3. 6. 108-9

[1800] What linsey-woolsey hast thou to speak to us again?

4. 1. 11-12

[1801] Tongue, I must put you into a butter-woman's mouth.

4. 1. 41-42

[1802] Is it possible he should know what he is, and be that he
is?

4. 1. 44-45

[1803] Three great oaths would scarce make that be believed.

4. 1. 58-59

[1804] Keep him dark and safely locked.

4. 1. 102-3

[1805] My mother told me just how he would woo
As if she sat in's heart. She says all men
Have the like oaths.

4. 2. 69-71

[1806] He has much worthy blame laid upon him.

4. 3. 5

[1807] What a past-saving slave is this!

4. 3. 135

[1808] His brains are forfeit to the next tile that falls.

4. 3. 185

He is lousy.   [1809]

4. 3. 188

I knew [him to] be a dangerous and lascivious boy, who is   [1810]
a whale to virginity, and devours up all the fry it finds.

4. 3. 212-13

After he scores he never pays the score.   [1811]

4. 3. 216

I could endure anything before but a cat, and now he's a   [1812]
cat to me.

4. 3. 229-30

He will steal, sir, an egg out of a cloister.   [1813]

4. 3. 241

He professes not keeping of oaths; in breaking 'em he is   [1814]
stronger than Hercules.

4. 3. 242-44

He will lie, sir, with such volubility that you would think   [1815]
truth were a fool.

4. 3. 244-45

Drunkenness is his best virtue, for he will be swine-   [1816]
drunk.

4. 3. 245-46

In his sleep he does little harm, save to his bedclothes   [1817]
about him.

4. 3. 246-48

He has everything that an honest man should not have;   [1818]
what an honest man should have, he has nothing.

4. 3. 250-52

[1819] He hath out-villain'd villainy so far that the rarity redeems him.

4. 3. 264-65

[1820] He excels his brother for a coward, yet his brother is reputed one of the best that is.

4. 3. 279-80

[1821] In a retreat he outruns any lackey; marry, in coming on he has the cramp.

4. 3. 280-82

[1822] [He is] a snipp'd-taffeta fellow!

4. 5. 1-2

[1823] [His] villainous saffron would have made all the unbak'd and doughy youth of a nation in his colour.

4. 5. 2-4

[1824] He has no pace, but runs where he will.

4. 5. 64

[1825] [You are] now, sir, muddied in Fortune's mood, and smell somewhat strong of her strong displeasure.

5. 2. 4-5

[1826] Foh! Prithee stand away. A paper from Fortune's closestool!

5. 2. 16-17

[1827] Here is a pur of Fortune's, sir, or of Fortune's cat that has fall'n into the unclean fishpond of her displeasure.

5. 2. 19-21

[1828] Use the carp as you may, for he looks like a poor, decayed, ingenious, foolish, rascally knave.

5. 2. 22-24

[She] was in mine eye the dust that did offend it. [1829]

5. 3. 54-55

I will buy me a son-in-law in a fair. I'll none of him. [1830]

5. 3. 146-47

Lay a more noble thought upon mine honour [1831]
Than for to think that I would sink it here.

5. 3. 179-80

She was a common gamester to the camp. [1832]

5. 3. 187

I saw the man today, if man he be. [1833]

5. 3. 202

You boggle shrewdly; every feather starts you. [1834]

5. 3. 231

This woman's an easy glove, my lord; she goes off and on [1835]
at pleasure.

5. 3. 271-72

I think thee now some common customer. [1836]

5. 3. 280

She does abuse to our ears. [1837]

5. 3. 288

Let thy curtsies alone, they are scurvy ones. [1838]

5. 3. 317-18

Antony and Cleopatra

[1839] I had rather heat my liver with drinking.

1. 2. 23

[1840] O, let him marry a woman that cannot go, and let her die too, and give him a worse, and let worse follow worse, till the worst of all follow him laughing to his grave, fifty-fold a cuckold!

1. 2. 60-64

[1841] It is a deadly sorrow to behold a foul knave uncuckolded.

1. 2. 69-70

[1842] We cannot call her winds and waters sighs and tears; they are greater storms and tempests than almanacs can report.

1. 2. 145-47

[1843] No more light answers.

1. 2. 174

[1844] Pray you stand farther from me.

1. 3. 18

I should take you for idleness itself.   [1845]

1. 3. 92-93

                    'Tis sweating labour,   [1846]
To bear such idleness so near the heart.

1. 3. 93-94

[You're] a man who is the abstract of all faults   [1847]
That all men follow.

1. 4. 9-10

[You] reel the streets at noon, and stand the buffet with   [1848]
knaves that smells of sweat.

1. 4. 20-23

We do bear so great weight in his lightness.   [1849]

1. 4. 25

He fill'd his vacancy with his voluptuousness.   [1850]

1. 4. 25-26

                    Thou didst drink   [1851]
The stale of horses, and the gilded puddle
Which beasts would cough at.

1. 4. 61-63

                    'Tis well for thee   [1852]
That, being unseminar'd, thy freer thoughts
May not fly forth.

1. 5. 10-12

Die a beggar.   [1853]

1. 5. 65

I will give thee bloody teeth.   [1854]

1. 5. 70

[1855] Tie up the libertine in a field of feasts.

1. 5. 23

[1856] I should once name you derogately.

2. 2. 33-34

[1857] You praise yourself,
By laying defects of judgment to me; but
You patch'd up your excuses.

2. 2. 54-56

[1858] Much uncurbable, her garboils.

2. 2. 67

[1859] [You] considerate stone!

2. 2. 110

[1860] This was but as a fly by an eagle.

2. 2. 181

[1861] As well a woman with an eunuch play'd.

2. 5. 5

[1862] My bended hook shall pierce
Their slimy jaws.

2. 5. 12-13

[1863] The gold I give thee will I melt and pour
Down thy ill-uttering throat.

2. 5. 34-35

[1864] There's no goodness in thy face.

2. 5. 37

[1865] [You are] like a Fury crown'd with snakes,
Not like a formal man.

2. 5. 40-41

I have a mind to strike thee ere thou speak'st. [1866]

2. 5. 42

The most infectious pestilence upon thee! [1867]

2. 5. 61

              Hence, [1868]
Horrible villain, or I'll spurn thine eyes
Like balls before me; I'll unhair thy head,
Thou shalt be whipp'd with wire, and stew'd in brine,
Smarting in lingering pickle.

2. 5. 62-66

Rogue, thou hast liv'd too long. [1869]

2. 5. 73

            Go get thee hence, [1870]
Hadst thou Narcissus in thy face, to me
Thou wouldst appear most ugly.

2. 5. 95-97

She creeps. [1871]

3. 3. 18

Their tongues rot that speak against us! [1872]

3. 7. 15-16

Experience, manhood, honour, ne'er before [1873]
Did violate so itself.

3. 10. 23-24

Think, and die. [1874]

3. 13. 2

           Thou art so leaky [1875]
That we must leave thee to thy sinking.

3. 13. 63-64

[1876]   You have been a boggler ever.

3. 13. 110

[1877]   I am sure,
Though you can guess what temperance should be,
You know not what it is.

3. 13. 120-22

[1878]   We'll beat 'em into bench-holes.

4. 7. 9

[1879]   [Thou] greatest spot of all thy sex!

4. 12. 35-36

[1880]   [You are] commanded
By such poor passion as the maid that milks,
And does the meanest chores.

4. 15. 73-75

[1881]   [You are] of no more trust
Than love that's hir'd.

5. 2. 153-54

[1882]   Prithee go hence,
Or I shall show the cinders of my spirits
Through the ashes of my chance.

5. 2. 171-73

[1883]   [You are] mechanic slaves
With greasy aprons, rules, and hammers.

5. 2. 208-9

[1884]   In their thick breaths,
Rank of gross diet, shall we be enclouded,
And forc'd to drink their vapour.

5. 2. 210-12

As You Like It

His animals on his dunghills are as much bound to him as I. [1885]

> 1. 1. 14-15

Thou hast railed on thyself. [1886]

> 1. 1. 61-62

I will no further offend you than becomes me for my good. [1887]

> 1. 1. 79-80

Her benefits are mightily misplaced. [1888]

> 1. 2. 33-34

Hath not Fortune sent in this fool to cut off the argument? [1889]

> 1. 2. 44-45

The dullness of the fool is the whetstone of the wits. [1890]

> 1. 2. 52-53

How prove you that in the great heap of your knowledge? [1891]

> 1. 2. 64-65

[1892]   Well said! That was laid on with a trowel.

1. 2. 98

[1893]   Where is this young gallant that is so desirous to lie with his mother earth?

1. 2. 188-89

[1894]   [I've] not one [word] to throw at a dog.

1. 3. 3

[1895]   If [your] purgation did consist in words,
[You] are as innocent as grace itself.

1. 3. 49-50

[1896]   Your mistrust cannot make me a traitor.

1. 3. 52

[1897]   What shall I call thee when thou art a man?

1. 3. 119

[1898]   [You're] like the toad, ugly and venomous.

2. 1. 13

[1899]   Sweep on you fat and greasy citizens!

2. 1. 55

[1900]   Thou prun'st a rotten tree.

2. 3. 63

[1901]   How many actions most ridiculous
Hast thou been drawn to by thy fantasy?

2. 4. 27-28

[1902]   It grows something stale with me.

2. 4. 59

That they call compliment is like th' encounter of two   [1903]
dog-apes.

                              2. 5. 23-24

I think he be transform'd into a beast,   [1904]
For I can nowhere find him like a man.

                              2. 7. 1-2

His brain is as dry as the remainder biscuit after a voy-   [1905]
age.

                              2. 7. 38-40

All th' embossed sores and headed evils   [1906]
That thou with licence of free foot hast caught
Wouldst thou disgorge into the general world.

                              2. 7. 67-69

Of what kind should this cock come of?   [1907]

                              2. 7. 91

In civility thou seem'st so empty.   [1908]

                              2. 7. 94

Truly thou art damned, like an ill-roasted egg, all on one   [1909]
side.

                              3. 2. 36-37

Most shallow man! Thou worms-meat in respect of a   [1910]
good piece of flesh indeed!

                              3. 2. 63-64

God help thee, shallow man! God make incision in thee,   [1911]
thou art raw!

                              3. 2. 69-70

That is another simple sin in you, to offer to get your   [1912] living by the copulation of cattle.

3. 2. 76-78

[1913] [You're] a crooked-pated old cuckoldly ram, out of all reasonable match.

3. 2. 80-81

[1914] This is a very false gallop of verses; why do you infect yourself with them?

3. 2. 111-12

[1915] You'll be rotten ere you be half ripe.

3. 2. 117

[1916] Is his head worth a hat? Or his chin worth a beard?

3. 2. 202-3

[1917] I found him under a tree like a dropped acorn.

3. 2. 230-31

[1918] Let's meet as little as we can.

3. 2. 253

[1919] I do desire we may be better strangers.

3. 2. 254

[1920] 'Tis a fault I will not change for your best virtue.

3. 2. 278

[1921] By my troth, I was seeking for a fool when I found you.

3. 2. 280-81

[1922] I am glad of your departure. Adieu good Monsieur Melancholy.

3. 2. 288-89

[1923] To cast away honesty upon a foul slut were to put good meat into an unclean dish.

3. 3. 31-32

Praised be the gods for thy foulness; sluttishness may [1924]
come hereafter.

3. 3. 34-35

His kisses are Judas's own children. [1925]

3. 4. 7-8

He hath bought a pair of cast lips of Diana. A nun of [1926]
winter's sisterhood kisses not more religiously, the very
ice of chastity is in them.

3. 4. 14-16

For his verity in love, I do think him as concave as a [1927]
covered goblet or a worm-eaten nut.

3. 4. 22-23

[You're] the confirmer of false reckonings. [1928]

3. 4. 29

I do frown on thee with all my heart, [1929]
And if mine eyes can wound, now let them kill thee.

3. 5. 15-16

I see no more in you than in the ordinary [1930]
Of Nature's sale-work.

3. 5. 42-43

        'Tis such fools as you [1931]
That makes the world full of ill-favour'd children.

3. 5. 52-53

Sell when you can, you are not for all markets. [1932]

3. 5. 60

[1933]   [You are] falser than vows made in wine.

3. 5. 73

[1934]   You have sold your own lands to see other men's.

4. 1. 21-22

[1935]   You lisp and wear strange suits.

4. 1. 31-32

[1936]   I had as lief be wooed of a snail.

4. 1. 50

[1937]   Men are April when they woo, December when they wed.

4. 1. 139-40

[1938]   You met your wife's wit going to your neighbour's bed.

4. 1. 159-60

[1939]   Let her never nurse her child herself, for she will breed it like a fool.

4. 1. 165-67

[1940]   I think you the most pathetical break-promise, and the most hollow lover that may be chosen out of the gross band of the unfaithful.

4. 1. 181-85

[1941]   You have simply misused our sex in your love-prate.

4. 1. 191-92

[1942]   [You're] conceived of spleen and born of madness.

4. 1. 202-3

[1943]   She has a leathern hand,
A freestone-colour'd hand. I verily did think
That her old gloves were on, but 'twas her hands.

4. 3. 24-26

'Tis a boisterous and a cruel style.   [1944]

4. 3. 31

Women's gentle brain could not drop forth such giant-   [1945]
rude invention.

4. 3. 33-34

Love hath made thee a tame snake.   [1946]

4. 3. 69-70

Take a good heart, and counterfeit to be a man.   [1947]

4. 3. 173-74

I will kill thee a hundred and fifty ways. Therefore trem-   [1948]
ble and depart.

5. 1. 55-57

I count it but time lost to hear such a foolish song.   [1949]

5. 3. 43-44

God mend your voices.   [1950]

5. 3. 44-45

Here comes a pair of very strange beasts, which in all   [1951]
tongues are called fools.

5. 4. 36-38

[You] motley-minded gentleman!   [1952]

5. 4. 40-41

[You] quarrel in print, by the book; as you have books for [1953]
good manners.

5. 4. 89-90

The Comedy of Errors

[1954] I shall break that merry sconce of yours
That stands on tricks when I am indispos'd.

1. 2. 79-80

[1955] Dost thou jeer and flout me in the teeth?

2. 2. 22

[1956] When the sun shines let foolish gnats make sport.

2. 2. 30

[1957] If you will jest with me, know my aspect,
And fashion your demeanour to my looks,
Or I will beat this method in your sconce.

2. 2. 32-34

[1958] There's many a man hath more hair than wit.

2. 2. 81-82

[1959] Thou drone, thou snail, thou slug, thou sot.

2. 2. 194

[1960] If thou art chang'd to aught, 'tis to an ass.

2. 2. 199

I think thou art an ass. [1961]

3. 1. 15

Mome, malthorse, capon, coxcomb, idiot, patch! [1962]

3. 1. 32

She would have me as a beast, not that I being a beast [1963]
she would have me, but that she being a very beastly
creature lays claim to me.

3. 2. 84-86

I have but lean luck in the match, and yet is she a won- [1964]
drous fat marriage.

3. 2. 90-91

She's the kitchen wench, and all grease, and I know not [1965]
what use to put her to but to make a lamp of her, and
run from her by her own light.

3. 2. 93-96

I warrant her rags and the tallow in them will burn a [1966]
Poland winter.

3. 2. 96-97

If she lives till doomsday she'll burn a week longer than [1967]
the whole world.

3. 2. 97-98

[She is] swart like my shoe, but her face nothing like so [1968]
clean kept.

3. 2. 100-1

She sweats, a man may go over-shoes in the grime of it. [1969]

3. 2. 101-2

No longer from head to foot than from hip to hip, she is [1970] spherical, like a globe; I could find out countries in her.

3. 2. 111-13

[1971] In what part of her body stands Ireland?
Marry, sir, in her buttocks; I found it out by the bogs.

3. 2. 114-16

[1972] Where Scotland?
I found it out by the barrenness, hard in the palm of the hand.

3. 2. 118-19

[1973] Where France?
In her forehead, armed and reverted, making war against her heir.

3. 2. 120-22

[1974] Where England?
I looked for the chalky cliffs, but I could find no whiteness in them. But I guess it stood in her chin, by the salt rheum that ran between France and it.

3. 2.123-27

[1975] Where Spain?
Faith, I saw it not; but I felt it hot in her breath.

3. 2. 128-30

[1976] Where America, the Indies?
O, sir, upon her nose, all o'er-embellished with rubies, carbuncles, sapphires, declining their rich aspect to the hot breath of Spain, who sent whole armadoes of carracks to be ballast at her nose.

3. 2. 131-36

[1977] Where stood Belgia, the Netherlands?
O, sir, I did not look so low.

3. 2. 137-38

As from a bear a man would run for life, [1978]
So fly I from her that would be my wife.

3. 2. 153-54

Hc is deformed, crooked, old and sere, [1979]
Ill-fac'd, worse bodied, shapeless everywhere;
Vicious, ungentle, foolish, blunt, unkind,
Stigmatical in making, worse in mind.

4. 2. 19-22

He's in Tartar limbo, worse than hell. [1980]
A devil in an everlasting garment hath him,
One whose hard heart is button'd up with steel;
A fiend, a fury, pitiless and rough,
A wolf, nay worse, a fellow all in buff;
A back-friend, a shoulder-clapper, one that counter
        mands
The passages of alleys, creeks and narrow lands;
A hound that runs counter, and yet draws dry-foot well,
One that, before the judgment, carries poor souls to hell.

4. 2. 32-40

Thou art sensible in nothing but blows, and so is an ass. [1981]

4. 4. 25-26

Dissembling harlot, thou art false in all, [1982]
And art confederate with a damned pack
To make a loathsome abject scorn of me.

4. 4. 99-101

The fiend is strong within him. [1983]

4. 4. 105

[What a] mountain of mad flesh! [1984]

4. 4. 152

Coriolanus

[1985] What's the matter, you dissentious rogues
That, rubbing the poor itch of your opinion,
Make yourselves scabs?

1. 1. 163-65

[1986] He that will give good words to thee will flatter
Beneath abhorring.

1. 1. 166-67

[1987]   He that trusts to you,
Where he should find you lions, finds you hares;
Where foxes, geese.

1. 1. 169-71

[1988]   You are no surer, no,
Than is the coal of fire upon the ice,
Or hailstone in the sun.

1. 1. 171-73

[1989]   Who deserves greatness,
Deserves your hate; and your affections are
A sick man's appetite, who desires most that

Which would increase his evil.

> 1. 1. 175-78

> He that depends [1990]
Upon your favours, swims with fins of lead,
And hews down oaks with rushes.

> 1. 1. 178-80

With every minute you do change a mind, [1991]
And call him noble that was now your hate,
Him vile that was your garland.

> 1. 1. 181-83

They'll sit by th' fire, and presume to know what's done [1992]
i' th' Capitol.

> 1. 1. 190-91

You cowards, you were got in fear. [1993]

> 1. 3. 33

She will but disease our better mirth. [1994]

> 1. 3. 103-4

All the contagion of the south light on you! [1995]

> 1. 4. 30

> Boils and plagues [1996]
Plaster you o'er, that you may be abhorr'd
Farther than seen, and one infect another
Against the wind a mile!

> 1. 4. 31-34

> You souls of geese, [1997]
That bear the shapes of men, how have you run
From slaves that apes would beat!

> 1. 4. 34-36

[1998]   By the fires of heaven, I'll leave the foe
And make my wars on you.

1. 4. 39-40

[1999]   There is the man of my soul's hate.

1. 5. 10

[2000]   I do hate thee worse than a promise-breaker.

1. 8. 1-2

[2001]   Not Afric owns a serpent I abhor more than thy fame and
envy.

1. 8. 3-4

[2002]   [You] fusty plebeians!

1. 9. 7

[2003]   Your abilities are too infant-like for doing much alone.

2. 1. 36-37

[2004]   [You] brace of unmeriting, proud, violent, testy magistrates!

2. 1. 42-43

[2005]   [You are] one that converses more with the buttock of the
night than with the forehead of the morning.

2. 1. 50-52

[2006]   I find the ass in compound with the major part of your
syllables.

2. 1. 57-58

[2007]   They lie deadly that tell you have good faces.

2. 1. 60-61

[2008]   You wear out a good wholesome forenoon in hearing a
cause between an orange-wife and a faucet-seller, and

then rejourn the controversy of threepence to a second
day of audience.

2. 1. 69-72

When you are hearing a matter between party and party,   [2009]
if you chance to be pinched with the colic, you make
faces like mummers, set up the bloody flag against all
patience, and, in roaring for a chamber-pot, dismiss the
controversy bleeding, the more entangled by your hearing.

2. 1. 72-77

All the peace you make in their cause is calling both the   [2010]
parties knaves.

2. 1. 77-79

Our very priests must become mockers, if they shall   [2011]
encounter such ridiculous subjects as you are.

2. 1. 83-84

When you speak best unto the purpose, it is not worth   [2012]
the wagging of your beards; and your beards deserve not
so honourable a grave as to stuff a botcher's cushion, or
to be entombed in an ass's pack-saddle.

2. 1. 84-87

In a cheap estimation, [he] is worth all your predecessors   [2013]
since Deucalion, though peradventure some of the best of
'em were hereditary hangmen.

2. 1. 90-92

More of your conversation would infect my brain.   [2014]

2. 1. 93-94

[You] old crabtrees!   [2015]

2.1 . 187

[2016]   Never would [I] beg their stinking breaths.

2. 1. 230-34

[2017]   In human action and capacity, [they are] of no more soul nor fitness for the world than camels.

2. 1. 247-49

[2018]   If they love they know not why, they hate upon no better a ground.

2. 2. 10-11

[2019]   He seeks their hate with greater devotion than they can render it him.

2. 2. 18-19

[2020]   Your wit will not so soon out as another man's will; 'tis strongly wedged up in a blockhead: but if it were at liberty, 'twould, sure, southward, to lose itself in a fog, where, being three parts melted away with rotten dews, the fourth would return for conscience' sake, to help to get thee a wife.

2. 3. 27-34

[2021]   Bid them wash their faces, and keep their teeth clean.

2. 3. 62-63

[2022]   Behold, these are the tongues o' th' common mouth!

3. 1. 21-22

[2023]   [You] time-pleasers, flatterers, foes to nobleness!

3. 1. 44

[2024]   [You] mutable, rank-scented meiny [crew]!

3. 1. 65

[2025]   Hear you this Triton of the minnows?

3. 1. 88

Hence rotten thing! or I shall shake thy bones out of thy   [2026]
garments.

> 3. 1. 177-78

He's a disease that must be cut away.   [2027]

> 3. 1. 292

You common cry of curs! whose breath I hate   [2028]
As reek o' th' rotten fens, whose loves I prize
As the dead carcasses of unburied men
That do corrupt my air.

> 3. 3. 120-23

The red pestilence strike all!   [2029]

> 4. 1. 13

I would the gods had nothing else to do   [2030]
But to confirm my curses!

> 4. 2. 45-46

Follow your function, go, and batten on cold bits.   [2031]

> 4. 5. 34

[I'll] scotch [you] and notch [you] like a carbonado.   [2032]

> 4. 5. 191-92

If he had been cannibally given, he might have broiled   [2033]
and eaten him too.

> 4. 5. 193-94

Breath of garlic-eaters!   [2034]

> 4. 6. 99

[Be] mocked for valiant ignorance, and perish constant   [2035]
fools.

> 4. 6. 105-6

[2036] The people deserve such pity of him as the wolf does of the shepherds.

4. 6. 110-12

[2037] You are they that made the air unwholesome when you cast your stinking greasy caps in hooting.

4. 6. 130-32

[2038] You are the musty chaff, and you are smelt above the moon.

5. 1. 31-32

[2039] For such things as you, I can scarce think there's any, y'are so slight.

5. 2. 101-2

[2040] For you, be that you are, long; and your misery increase with your age!

5. 2. 104-5

[2041] The benefit which thou shalt reap is such a name whose repetition will be dogg'd with curses.

5. 3. 142-44

[2042] The tartness of his face sours ripe grapes.

5. 4. 17-18

[2043] There is no more mercy in him than there is milk in a male tiger.

5. 4. 28-29

Cymbeline

He is a thing too bad for bad report.   [2044]

                           1. 1. 16-17

How fine this tyrant can tickle where she wounds!   [2045]

                          1. 2. 15-16

Thou'rt poison to my blood.   [2046]

                          1. 2. 59

O disloyal thing, thou heap'st a year's age on me!   [2047]

                          1. 2. 62-64

I chose an eagle, and did avoid a puttock.   [2048]

                          1. 2. 70-71

You reek as a sacrifice: where air comes out, air comes   [2049]
    in:
There's none abroad so wholesome as that you vent.

                          1. 3. 2-4

You had measur'd how long a fool you were upon the   [2050]
ground.

                          1. 3. 22-23

[2051] Her beauty and her brain go not together.

1. 3. 28-29

[2052] I have seen small reflection of her wit.

1. 3. 29-30

[2053] She shines not upon fools, lest the reflection should hurt her.

1. 3. 31-32

[2054] The fall of an ass is no great hurt.

1. 3. 35-36

[2055] My father, like the tyrannous breathing of the north, shakes all our buds from growing.

1. 4. 35-37

[2056] She's outpriz'd by a trifle.

1. 5. 83-84

[2057] You are a great deal abus'd in too bold a persuasion.

1. 5. 118-19

[2058] If you buy ladies' flesh at a million a dram, you cannot preserve it from tainting.

1. 5. 139-41

[2059] [It] exceeds in goodness the hugeness of your unworthy thinking.

1. 5. 149-50

[2060] Here comes a flattering rascal.

1. 6. 27

[2061] Every day that comes comes to decay a day's work in him.

1. 6. 56-57

[These are] diseas'd ventures that play with all infirmities   [2062]
for gold.

> 1. 7. 123-24

Such boil'd stuff as well might poison poison!   [2063]

> 1. 7. 125-26

Away, I do condemn mine ears, that have so long at-   [2064]
tended thee.

> 1. 7. 141-42

He shall think it fit to expound his beastly mind to us.   [2065]

> 1. 7. 150-53

A whoreson jackanapes [that] takes me up for swearing,   [2066]
as if I borrowed mine oaths of him, and might not spend
them at my pleasure.

> 2. 1. 3-6

You are cock and capon too, and you crow, cock, with   [2067]
your comb on.

> 2. 1. 25-26

It is fit I should commit offence to my inferiors.   [2068]

> 2. 1. 30-31

You are a fool granted, therefore your issues being foolish   [2069]
do not derogate.

> 2. 1. 48-49

That such a crafty devil as his mother should yield the   [2070]
world this ass!

> 2. 1. 54-55

I shall unfold equal discourtesy to your best kindness.   [2071]

> 2. 3. 97-98

[2072]   Learn now, for all,
That I, which know my heart, do here pronounce,
By th' very truth of it,
I care not for you,
And am so near the lack of charity
(To accuse myself) I hate you.

                                        2. 3. 107-11

[2073] The south-fog rot him!

                                        2. 3. 132

[2074]   His meanest garment,
That ever hath but clipp'd his body, is dearer
In my respect, than all the hairs above thee.

                                        2. 3. 134-36

[2075] I am sprited with a fool.

                                        2. 3. 140

[2076] All the fiends of hell divide themselves between you!

                                        2. 4. 129-30

[2077] [His] ambition swell'd so much that it did almost stretch
the sides o' th' world.

                                        3. 1. 50-52

[2078] Our crows shall fare the better for you.

                                        3. 1. 83-84

[2079] [She's] rustling in unpaid-for silk.

                                        3. 3. 24

[2080] [Here's] a cell of ignorance, travelling a-bed.

                                        3. 3. 33

[2081] One but painted thus would be interpreted a thing

perplex'd beyond self-explication.

3. 4. 6-8

Thou art the pandar to her dishonour. [2082]

3. 4. 30-31

[His] tongue
Outvenoms all the worms of Nile. [2083]

3. 4. 33-34

Men's vows are women's traitors! [2084]

3. 4. 54

Why hast thou abus'd so many miles, with a pretence? [2085]

3. 4. 103-4

Talk thy tongue weary. [2086]

3. 4. 113

[I'll] no more ado with that harsh, noble, simple nothing, [2087]
whose love-suit hath been to me as fearful as a siege.

3. 4. 132-35

From [his] so many weights of baseness cannot a dram of [2088]
worth be drawn.

3. 5. 89-90

The bitterness of it I now belch from my heart. [2089]

3. 5. 137-38

[Thou] imperseverant thing! [2090]

4. 1. 15-16

Thy words I grant are bigger: for I wear not my dagger in [2091]
my mouth.

4. 2. 78-79

[2092] Thou art some fool, I am loath to beat thee.

4. 2. 85-86

[2093] [He was] a fool, an empty purse,
There was no money in't: not Hercules
Could have knock'd out his brains, for he had none.

4. 2. 113-15

[2094] His humour was nothing but mutation, ay, and that from one bad thing to worse.

4. 2. 132-34

[2095] This body hath a tail more perilous than the head.

4. 2. 144-45

[2096] [You're] the geck and scorn o' th' other's villainy.

5. 4. 67-68

[2097] No more, you petty spirits of region low, offend our hearing.

5. 4. 93-94

[2098] Away: no farther with your din express impatience, lest you stir up mine.

5. 4. 111-12

[2099] His celestial breath was sulphurous to smell.

5. 4. 114-15

[2100] 'Tis such stuff as madmen tongue, and brain not.

5. 4. 146-47

[2101] Fiend! Most credulous fool, egregious murderer, thief, any thing that's due to all the villains past, in being, to come!

5. 5. 210-13

Hamlet

Frailty, thy name is woman. [2102]

1. 2. 146

[You have] a truant disposition. [2103]

1. 2. 169

      Do not [2104]
Show me the steep and thorny way to heaven,
Whiles like a puff'd and reckless libertine
[Your]self the primrose path of dalliance treads.

1. 3. 47-50

Do not believe his vows; for they are brokers [2105]
Breathing like sanctified and pious bawds
The better to beguile.

1. 3. 127-31

They clepe us drunkards, and with swinish phrase [2106]
Soil our addition.

1. 4. 19-20

[You] vicious mole of nature! [2107]

1. 4. 24

[2108]   Something is rotten in the state of Denmark.

1. 4. 90

[2109]   [You're] a wretch whose natural gifts were poor.

1. 5. 51

[2110]   [Your] lust, though to a radiant angel link'd,
Will sate itself in a celestial bed
And prey on garbage.

1. 5. 55-57

[2111]   [You are] a most instant tetter [scab] bark'd about
Most lazar-like, with vile and loathsome crust.

1. 5. 71-72

[2112]   One may smile, and smile, and be a villain.

1. 5. 108

[2113]   Well said, old mole. Canst work i' th' earth so fast?

1. 5. 170

[2114]   He is open to incontinency.

2. 1. 30

[2115]   Your bait of falsehood takes this carp of truth.

2. 1. 63

[2116]   Brevity is the soul of wit,
And tediousness the limbs and outward flourishes.

2. 2. 90-91

[2117]   More matter with less art.

2. 2. 94

[2118]   This effect defective comes by cause.

2. 2. 103

You are a fishmonger.   [2119]

                                    2. 2. 174

They have a plentiful lack of wit, together with most weak   [2120]
hams.

                                    2. 2. 198-99

You yourself, sir, shall grow old as I am if like a crab you   [2121]
could go backward.

                                    2. 2. 203-4

I will most humbly take my leave of you.   [2122]
You cannot, sir, take from me anything that I will not
more willingly part withal.

                                    2. 2. 213-16

It appeareth nothing to me but a foul and pestilent con-   [2123]
gregation of vapours.

                                    2. 2. 301-3

What is this quintessence of dust?   [2124]

                                    2. 2. 308

O, there has been much throwing about of brains.   [2125]

                                    2. 2. 356

Came each actor on his ass.   [2126]

                                    2. 2. 391

[He], like a neutral to his will and matter,   [2127]
Did nothing.

                                    2. 2. 477-78

He's for a jig or a tale of bawdry, or he sleeps.   [2128]

                                    2. 2. 96

[2129]   [You're] a dull and muddy-mettled rascal.

2. 2. 562

[2130]   [You are] pigeon-liver'd and lack gall.

2. 2. 573

[2131]   I should ha' fatted all the region kites
With this slave's offal.

2. 2. 575-76

[2132]   Get thee to a nunnery.

3. 1. 121

[2133]   [He is] very proud, revengeful, ambitious, with more
offences at [his] beck than [he] has thoughts to put them
in, imagination to give them shape, or time to act them
in.

3. 1. 124-27

[2134]   What should such fellows as [he] do crawling between
earth and heaven?

3. 1. 128-29

[2135]   Let the doors be shut upon him, that he may play the fool
nowhere but in's own house.

3. 1. 133-34

[2136]   If thou dost marry, I'll give thee this plague for thy dowry.

3. 1. 136-37

[2137]   If thou wilt needs marry, marry a fool; for wise men know
well enough what monsters you make of them.

3. 1. 139-41

[2138]   God hath given you one face and you make yourselves
another.

3. 1. 144-45

It offends me to the soul to hear a robustious periwig-
pated fellow tear a passion to tatters.   [2139]
> 3. 2. 8-10

[These] groundlings for the most part are capable of   [2140]
nothing but inexplicable dumb-shows and noise.
> 3. 2. 11-12

It out-Herods Herod.   [2141]
> 3. 2. 14

Though it makes the unskilful laugh, [it] cannot but   [2142]
make the judicious grieve.
> 3. 2. 25-26

[They] have so strutted and bellowed that I have thought   [2143]
some of Nature's journeymen had made men, and not
made them well.
> 3. 2. 29-34

[Here is] some quantity of barren spectators!   [2144]
> 3. 2. 41

That's villainous, and shows a most pitiful ambition in   [2145]
the fool that uses it.
> 3. 2. 43-45

Let the candied tongue lick absurd pomp.   [2146]
> 3. 2. 60

[Thou art] a pipe for Fortune's finger   [2147]
To sound what stop she please.
> 3. 2. 70-71

[Your] imaginations are as foul as Vulcan's stithy.   [2148]
> 3. 2. 83-84

[2149] I eat the air, promise-crammed. You cannot feed capons so.

3. 2. 93-94

[2150] Let the galled jade winch.

3. 2. 237

[2151] Leave thy damnable faces.

3. 2. 247

[2152] This courtesy is not of the right breed.

3. 2. 306-7

[2153] Do you think I am easier to be played on than a pipe?

3. 2. 360-61

[2154] I will speak daggers to her.

3. 2. 387

[2155] [Your] offence is rank, it smells to heaven.

3. 3. 36

[2156] Why, this is hire and salary, not revenge.

3. 3. 79

[2157] I took thee for thy better.

3. 4. 32

[2158]   Sense sure you have,
Else could you not have motion; but sure that sense
Is apoplex'd.

3. 4. 71-73

[2159]   What devil was't
That thus hath cozen'd you at hoodman-blind?

3. 4. 76-77

[You] live in the rank sweat of an enseamed bed,   [2160]
Stew'd in corruption, honeying and making love
Over the nasty sty!

                 3. 4. 91-94

Your bedded hair, like life in excrements,   [2161]
Start up and stand an end.

                 3. 4. 121-22

This is the very coinage of your brain.   [2162]

                 3. 4. 139

Assume a virtue if you have it not.   [2163]

                 3. 4. 161

I will trust [them] as I will adders fanged.   [2164]

                 3. 4. 205

Take you me for a sponge?   [2165]

                 4. 2. 13

A knavish speech sleeps in a foolish ear.   [2166]

                 4. 2. 22-23

[He is] in heaven. Send thither to see. If your messenger   [2167]
find him not there, seek him i' th'other place yourself.

                 4. 3. 33-35

[They are] muddied, thick, and unwholesome in their   [2168]
thoughts and whispers.

                 4. 5. 81-82

[You] have done but greenly in hugger-mugger.   [2169]

                 4. 5. 83-84

How cheerfully on the false trail they cry.   [2170]

                 4. 5. 109

[2171] Cudgel thy brains no more about it, for your dull ass will not mend his pace with beating.

5. 1. 56-57

[2172]   How absolute the knave is,
We must speak by the card, or equivocation will undo us.

5. 1. 133-34

[2173] Such bugs and goblins in my life!

5. 2. 22

[2174] [I am] benetted round with villainies.

5. 2. 29

[2175] Dost know this waterfly?

5. 2. 82-83

[2176] 'Tis a vice to know him.

5. 2. 85-86

[2177] [You are] spacious in the possession of dirt.

5. 2. 88-89

[2178] To divide him inventorially would dozy th'arithmetic of memory.

5. 2. 113-14

[2179] His purse is empty already, all's golden words are spent.

5. 2. 129-30

Henry IV, Part 1

Thou art so fat-witted with drinking of old sack, and [2180]
unbuttoning thee after supper, and sleeping upon
benches after noon, that thou hast forgotten to demand
that truly which thou wouldst truly know.

1. 2. 2-5

Unless hours were cups of sack, and minutes capons, [2181]
and clocks the tongues of bawds, and dials the signs of
leaping-houses, and the blessed sun himself a fair hot
wench in flame-coloured taffeta, I see no reason why thou
shouldst be so superfluous to demand the time of the
day.

1. 2. 7-12

Grace thou wilt have none, no, by my troth, not so much [2182]
as will serve to be prologue to an egg and butter.

1. 2. 17-21

Thou hast the most unsavoury similes. [2183]

1. 2. 77

[2184] I see a good amendment of life in thee, from praying to purse-taking.

1. 2. 99-100

[2185] O, if men were to be saved by merit, what hole in hell were hot enough for [you]?

1. 2. 104-5

[2186] How agrees the devil and thee about thy soul, that thou soldest him on Good Friday last, for a cup of Madeira and a cold capon's leg?

1. 2. 111-13

[2187] There's neither honesty, manhood, nor good fellowship in thee.

1. 2. 135-36

[2188] I know [you] to be as true-bred cowards as ever turned back.

1. 2. 177-78

[2189] I know you all, and will awhile uphold the unyok'd humour of your idleness.

1. 2. 190-91

[2190] [You] foul and ugly mists of vapours!

1. 2. 197-98

[2191] You tread upon my patience.

1. 3. 4

[2192] [What a] slovenly unhandsome corse!

1. 3. 43

[2193] With many holiday and lady terms
He question'd me.

1. 3. 45-46

To be so pester'd with a popinjay!   [2194]

1. 3. 49

He made me mad   [2195]
To see him shine so brisk, and smell so sweet,
And talk so like a waiting gentle-woman.

1. 3. 52-54

On the barren mountains let him starve!   [2196]

1. 3. 88

What, drunk with choler?   [2197]

1. 3. 127

[You're an] ingrate and canker'd.   [2198]

1. 3. 135

In the world's wide mouth   [2199]
Live scandaliz'd and foully spoken of.

1. 3. 151-52

Out upon this half-fac'd fellowship!   [2200]

1. 3. 206

I would have him poison'd with a pot of ale!   [2201]

1. 3. 230

[You] tie thine ear to no tongue but thine own.   [2202]

1. 3. 235

I am whipp'd and scourg'd with rods,   [2203]
Nettled, and stung with pismires, when I hear
Of this vile politician.

1. 3. 238-38

We leak in your chimney.   [2204]

2. 1. 19

[2205]   Your chamber-lye breeds fleas like a loach.

2. 1. 20

[2206]   Hast thou never an eye in thy head?

2. 1. 26-27

[2207]   [You] mad mustachio purple-hued maltworms!

2. 1. 73-74

[2208]   [You are] the veriest varlet that ever chewed with a tooth.

2. 2. 23-24

[2209]   Peace, ye fat guts!

2. 2. 31

[2210]   Hang thyself in thine own heir-apparent garters!

2. 2. 42

[2211]   [If] I have not ballads made on you all, and sung to filthy tunes, let a cup of sack be my poison.

2. 2. 43-45

[2212]   Whoreson caterpillars!

2. 2. 81

[2213]   Bacon-fed knaves!

2. 2. 81

[2214]   Ye fat chuffs!

2. 2. 84-85

[2215]   On, bacons, on!

2. 2. 85-86

[2216]   There's no more valour in [you] than in a wild duck.

2. 2. 95-96

[He] sweats to death,
And lards the lean earth as he walks along.   [2217]

> 2. 2. 103-4

Were't not for laughing I should pity him.   [2218]

> 2. 2. 105

How the fat rogue roared.   [2219]

> 2. 2. 106

You are a shallow cowardly hind, and you lie.   [2220]

> 2. 3. 15-16

What a lack-brain is this!   [2221]

> 2. 3. 16

I could brain him with his lady's fan.   [2222]

> 2. 3. 22-23

Such a dish of skim milk!   [2223]

> 2. 3. 33

A weasel hath not such a deal of spleen as you are toss'd   [2224]
with.

> 2. 3. 79-80

[I have been] with three or four loggerheads, amongst   [2225]
three or four hogsheads.

> 2. 4. 4-5

[You] have sounded the very base-string of humility.   [2226]

> 2. 4. 5-6

[You] leathern-jerkin, crystal-button, knot-pated, agate-   [2227]
ring, puke-stocking, caddis-garter, smooth-tongue, Span-
ish pouch!

> 2. 4. 68-70

[2228]   How now, wool-sack, what mutter you?

2. 4. 132

[2229]   These lies are like their father that begot them, gross as a
mountain, open, palpable.

2. 4. 220-21

[2230]   Thou clay-brained guts, thou knotty-pated fool, thou
whoreson obscene greasy tallow-catch!

2. 4. 221-23

[2231]   [You] sanguine coward, [you] bed-presser, [you] horse-
back-breaker, [you] huge hill of flesh!

2. 4. 237-39

[2232]   You starvelling, you eel-skin, you dried neat's-tongue,
you bull's-pizzle, you stock-fish—O for breath to utter
what is like thee!—you tailor's-yard, you sheath, you
bow-case, you vile standing tuck!

2. 4. 240-44

[2233]   What trick, what device, what starting-hole canst thou
now find out, to hide thee from this open and apparent
shame?

2. 4. 259-61

[2234]   How now, my sweet creature of bombast?

2. 4. 322-23

[2235]   Peace, good pintpot, peace, good tickle-brain.

2. 4. 392

[2236]   Thou art violently carried away from grace.

2. 4. 440

[2237]   There is a devil haunts thee in the likeness of an old fat man, a tun of man is thy companion.

2. 4. 441-42

Why dost thou converse with that trunk of humours, that [2238]
bolting-hutch of beastliness, that swollen parcel of
dropsies, that huge bombard of sack, that stuffed cloak-
bag of guts, that roasted Manningtree ox with the pudding in his belly, that reverend vice, that grey Iniquity,
that father ruffian, that vanity in years?

2. 4. 442-49

Wherein is he good, but to taste sack and drink it? [2239]
wherein neat and cleanly, but to carve a capon and eat
it? wherein cunning, but in craft? wherein crafty, but in
villainy? wherein villainous, but in all things? wherein
worthy, but in nothing?

2. 4. 449-53

[You] villainous abominable misleader of youth! [2240]

2. 4. 456

[You] old white-bearded Satan! [2241]

2. 4. 457

Thou art essentially a natural coward without instinct. [2242]

2. 4. 486-88

[You are] as fat as butter. [2243]

2. 4. 504

O, he is as tedious [2244]
As a tired horse, a railing wife,
Worse than a smoky house.

3. 1. 153-55

I had rather live [2245]
With cheese and garlic in a windmill, far,

Than feed on cates and have him talk to me
In any summer house in Christendom.

3. 1. 155-58

[2246]   Go, ye giddy goose.

3. 1. 223

[2247]   Thou art only mark'd for the hot vengeance and the rod of
heaven.

3. 2. 9-10

[2248]   Such inordinate and low desires,
Such poor, such bare, such lewd, such mean attempts,
Such barren pleasures, rude society,
As thou art match'd withal, and grafted to!

3. 2. 12-15

[2249]   [You] smiling pickthanks, and base newsmongers!

3. 2. 25

[2250]   [You] stand the push of every beardless vain comparative.

3. 2. 66-67

[2251]   [There's] not an eye but is a-weary of thy common sight.

3. 2. 87-88

[2252]   [Thou art] wither'd like an old apple-john.

3. 3. 4

[2253]   [Your] villainous company hath been the spite of me.

3. 3. 10

[2254]   Do thou amend thy face, and I'll amend my life.

3. 3. 23

[2255]   I make as good use of [your face] as many a man doth of a death's-head, or a *momento mori.*

> 3. 3. 28-29

I never see thy face but I think upon hell-fire.   [2256]

> 3. 3. 29-30

There's no more faith in thee than in a stewed prune.   [2257]

> 3. 3. 110-11

If [your girdle should break], how would thy guts fall   [2258]
about thy knees!

> 3. 3. 151-52

There's no room for faith, truth, nor honesty in this   [2259]
bosom of thine. It is all filled up with guts and midriff.

> 3. 3. 152-54

Thou whoreson impudent embossed rascal!   [2260]

> 3. 3. 155-56

Such toasts-and-butter, with hearts in their bellies no   [2261]
bigger than pins' heads.

> 4. 2. 20-22

[You are the] cankers of a calm world and a long peace.   [2262]

> 4. 2. 29-30

[You are] tattered prodigals lately come from swine-   [2263]
keeping, from eating draff and husks.

> 4. 2. 34-36

[You are] sick in the world's regard, wretched and low,   [2264]
A poor unminded outlaw sneaking home.

> 4. 3. 57-58

A fool go with thy soul, whither it goes!   [2265]

> 5. 3. 22

Henry IV, Part 2

[2266] [You] blunt monster with uncounted heads!

1. 0. 18

[2267] [He's] the dullest peasant in his camp.

1. 1. 114

[2268] The brain of this foolish-compounded clay, man, is not
able to invent anything that intends to laughter.

1. 2. 75-6

[2269] Thou whoreson mandrake, thou art fitter to be worn in
my cap than to wait at my heels.

1. 2. 13-15

[2270] I will sooner have a beard grow in the palm of my hand
than he shall get one off his cheek.

1. 2. 19-21

[2271] He may keep his own grace, but he's almost out of mine, I
can assure him.

1. 2. 27-28

[2272] The whoreson smooth-pates do now wear nothing but

high shoes and bunches of keys at their girdles.

1. 2. 37-39

[You] may sleep in security, for [you have] the horn of abundance, and the lightness of [your] wife shines through it.

[2273]

1. 2. 45-47

Well, the truth is you live in great infamy.

[2274]

1. 2. 135-36

Your means are very slender, and your waste is great.

[2275]

1. 2. 139-40

You are as a candle, the better part burnt out.

[2276]

1. 2. 155-56

Virtue is of so little regard in these costermongers' times that true valour is turned bearherd.

[2277]

1. 2. 167-69

All the gifts appertinent to man, as the malice of this age shapes them, are not worth a gooseberry.

[2278]

1. 2. 170-72

You that are old do measure the heat of our livers with the bitterness of your galls.

[2279]

1. 2. 172-75

Do you set down your name in the scroll of youth, that are written down old with all the characters of age? Have you not a moist eye, a dry hand, a yellow cheek, a white beard, a decreasing leg, an increasing belly? Is not your voice broken, your wind short, your chin double, your wit single, and every part about you blasted with antiquity? And will you yet call yourself young?

[2280]

1. 2. 177-84

[2281]   [You] repent not in ashes and sackcloth, but in new silk
and old sack.

1. 2. 196-98

[2282]   It was alway yet the trick of our English nation, if they
have a good thing, to make it too common.

1. 2. 214-16

[2283]   I were better to be eaten to death with a rust than to be
scoured to nothing with perpetual motion.

1. 2. 219-21

[2284]   [You] can get no remedy against this consumption of the
purse; borrowing only lingers and lingers it out, but the
disease is incurable.

1. 2. 237-39

[2285]   A pox of this gout! or a gout of this pox!

1. 2. 244-45

[2286]   [You act] with great imagination proper to madmen.

1. 3. 29-30

[2287]   [You] fortify in paper and in figures,
Using the names of men instead of men.

1. 3. 56-57

[2288]   So, so, thou common dog, didst thou disgorge
Thy glutton bosom.

1. 3. 97-98

[2289]   Thou wouldst eat thy dead vomit up,
And howl'st to find it.

1. 3. 99-100

[2290]   I have borne, and borne, and borne, and have been
fubbed off, and fubbed off, and fubbed off, from this day

to that day, that it is a shame to be thought on.

2. 1. 32-35

There is no honesty in such dealing, unless a woman   [2291]
should be made an ass, and a beast, to bear every
knave's wrong.

2. 1. 36-37

[You] arrant, malmsey-nose knave!   [2292]

2. 1. 38-39

You scullion! You rampallian! You fustilarian! I'll tickle   [2293]
your catastrophe!

2. 1. 58-59

He hath eaten me out of house and home, he hath put all   [2294]
my substance into that fat belly of his.

2. 1. 72-73

Fie! what man of good temper would endure this tempest   [2295]
of exclamation?

2. 1. 78-80

I am well acquainted with your manner of wrenching the   [2296]
true cause the false way.

2. 1. 107-9

I will not undergo this sneap without reply.   [2297]

2. 1. 121-22

Doth it not show vilely in [you] to desire small beer?   [2298]

2. 2. 5-6

What a disgrace is it to me to remember thy name!   [2299]

2. 2. 12-13

God knows whether those that bawl out the ruins of thy   [2300] linen shall inherit his kingdom.

2. 2. 23-24

[2301]   It shall serve, among wits of no higher breeding than thine.

2. 2. 34-35

[2302]   Look if the fat villain have not transformed him ape.

2. 2. 67-68

[2303]   What a maidenly man-at-arms are you become!

2. 2. 73-74

[2304]   I spied his eyes, and methought he had made two holes in the ale-wife's new petticoat, and so peeped through.

2. 2. 78-80

[2305]   You whoreson upright rabbit!

2. 2. 82

[2306]   Repent at idle times as thou mayst.

2. 2. 122-23

[2307]   Steep this letter in sack and make him eat it.

2. 2. 128-29

[2308]   Well, thus [they] play the fools with the time, and the spirits of the wise sit in the clouds and mock [them].

2. 2. 134-35

[2309]   Where sups he? Doth the old boar feed in the old frank?

2. 2. 138-39

[2310]   [You] dry, round, old, withered knights.

2. 4. 7-8

A pox damn you, you muddy rascal, is that all the comfort you give me? [2311]

2. 4. 39-40

If the cook help to make the gluttony, you help to make the diseases. [2312]

2. 4. 44-45

Hang yourself, you muddy conger [eel], hang yourself! [2313]

2. 4. 53

You are as rheumatic as two dry toasts. [2314]

2. 4. 55-56

Can a weak empty vessel bear such a huge full hogshead? [2315]

2. 4. 61-62

It is the foulmouth'dst rogue in England. [2316]

2. 4. 70

I scorn you, scurvy companion. What, you poor, base, rascally, cheating, lack-linen mate! Away, you mouldy rogue, away! [2317]

2. 4. 120-22

Away, you cutpurse rascal, you filthy bung, away! [2318]

2. 4. 125

Away, you bottle-ale rascal, you basket-hilt stale juggler, you! [2319]

2. 4. 127-29

Discharge yourself of our company. [2320]

2. 4. 134

[2321]   He lives upon mouldy stewed prunes and dried cakes.

> 2. 4. 142-43

[2322]   Feed, and be fat.

> 2. 4. 175

[2323]   I kiss thy neaf [first].

> 2. 4. 182

[2324]   I cannot endure such a fustian [bombastic] rascal.

> 2. 4. 185

[2325]   Alas, poor ape, how thou sweat'st!

> 2. 4. 213-14

[2326]   Thou whoreson little tidy Bartholomew boar-pig!

> 2. 4. 227

[2327]   Do not speak like a death's-head.

> 2. 4. 231

[2328]   A good shallow young fellow; he would have made a good pantryman, he would ha' chipped bread well.

> 2. 4. 234-35

[2329]   [Your] wit's as thick as Tewkesbury mustard.

> 2. 4. 237-38

[2330]   There's no more conceit in [you] than is in a mallet.

> 2. 4. 238-39

[2331]   Is it not strange that desire should so many years outlive performance?

> 2. 4. 258-59

Why, thou globe of sinful continents, what a life dost   [2332]
thou lead!

>   2. 4. 282-83

I am a gentleman, thou art a drawer.   [2333]

>   2. 4. 284-85

You whoreson candle-mine you! [lode of tallow fat]   [2334]

>   2. 4. 297

[Your] zeal burns in [your] nose.   [2335]

>   2. 4. 326-27

Answer, thou dead elm, answer.   [2336]

>   2. 4. 328

His face is Lucifer's privy-kitchen, where he doth nothing   [2337]
but roast malt-worms.

>   2. 4. 330-31

She is in hell already, and burns poor souls.   [2338]

>   2. 4. 335 3

She comes blubbered.   [2339]

>   2. 4. 386-87

O thou dull god, why li'st thou with the vile   [2340]
In loathsome beds?

>   3. 1. 15-16

Is thy name Mouldy?   [2341]

>   3. 2. 104

Thou art a very ragged Wart.   [2342]

>   3. 2. 140

[2343]   His apparel is built upon his back, and the whole frame stands upon pins.

3. 2. 142-43

[2344]   Wilt thou make as many holes in an enemy's battle as thou hast done in a woman's petticoat?

3. 2. 152-54

[2345]   Thou wilt be as valiant as the wrathful dove, or most magnanimous mouse.

3. 2. 157-58

[2346]   [You] present no mark to the enemy—the foeman may with as great aim level at the edge of a penknife.

3. 2. 260-62

[2347]   [You are] a little, lean, old, chopt, bald shot.

3. 2. 270

[2348]   Th' art a good scab.

3. 2. 271

[2349]   He is not his craft's master.

3. 2. 273

[2350]   Lord, Lord, how subject we old men are to this vice of lying!

3. 2. 296-98

[2351]   [You are] a man made after supper of a cheese-paring.

3. 2. 303-4

[2352]   When he was naked, he was for all the world like a forked radish, with a head fantastically carved upon it with a knife.

3. 2. 304-6

He was so forlorn, that his dimensions to any thick sight   [2353]
were invisible.

> 3. 2. 306-7

He was the very genius of famine, yet lecherous as a   [2354]
monkey, and the whores called him mandrake.

> 3. 2. 307-9

He came ever in the rearward of the fashion.   [2355]

> 3. 2. 309-10

You might have thrust him and all his apparel into an   [2356]
eel-skin.

> 3. 2. 319-20

I muse you make so slight a question.   [2357]

> 4. 1. 167

[I am] weary of [your] dainty and such picking grievances.   [2358]

> 4. 1. 197-98

You are too shallow, much too shallow,   [2359]
To sound the bottom of the after-times.

> 4. 2. 50-51

Rouse up fear and trembling, and do observance to my   [2360]
mercy.

> 4. 3. 14-15

It was more of his courtesy than your deserving.   [2361]

> 4. 3. 43

If you do not all show like gilt twopences to me, and I in   [2362]
the clear sky of fame o'ershine you as much as the full
moon doth the cinders of the element, which show like
pins' heads to her, believe not the word of the noble.

> 4. 3. 49-53

[2363] Thou like a kind fellow gavest thyself away *gratis*, and I thank thee for thee.

4. 3. 66-68

[2364] I, in my condition, shall speak better of you than you deserve.

4. 3. 82-83

[2365] I would you had but the wit.

4. 3. 84

[2366] Good faith, this same young sober-blooded boy doth not love me, nor a man cannot make him laugh; but that's no marvel, he drinks no wine.

4. 3. 85-88

[2367] There's never none of these demure boys come to any proof; for thin drink doth so over-cool their blood, and making many fish meals, that they fall into a kind of male green-sickness, and then when they marry they get wenches.

4. 3. 88-92

[2368] They are generally fools and cowards—which some of us should be too, but for inflammation.

4. 3. 92-94

[2369] His passions, like a whale on ground,
Confound themselves with working.

4. 4. 40-41

[2370] O polish'd perturbation!

4. 5. 22

[2371] Thy life did manifest thou lov'dst me not,
And thou wilt have me die assur'd of it.

4. 5. 104-5

Thou hid'st a thousand daggers in thy thoughts,   [2372]
Which thou hast whetted on thy stony heart,
To stab at half an hour of my life.

4. 5. 106-8

[You] apes of idleness!   [2373]

4. 5. 122

Purge you of your scum.   [2374]

4. 5. 123

[You are] a ruffian that will swear, drink, dance,   [2375]
Revel the night, rob, murder, and commit
The oldest sins the newest kind of ways.

4. 5. 124-26

I will not excuse you, you shall not be excused, excuses   [2376]
shall not be admitted, there is no excuse shall serve, you
shall not be excused.

5. 1. 4-6

They are arrant knaves, and will backbite.   [2377]

5. 1. 30

They have marvellous foul linen.   [2378]

5. 1. 31-32

They flock together in consent, like so many wild geese.   [2379]

5. 1. 67-68

It is certain that either wise bearing or ignorant carriage   [2380]
is caught, as men take diseases, one of another.

5. 1. 72-74

You shall see him laugh till his face be like a wet cloak ill   [2381]
laid up!

5. 1. 81-82

[2382]   You stand in coldest expectation.

5. 2. 31

[2383]   What wind blew you hither?

5. 3. 83

[2384]   Puff i' thy teeth, most recreant coward base!

5. 3. 89

[2385]   A *foutre* for the world and worldlings base!

5. 3. 96

[2386]   Shall dunghill curs confront the Helicons?

5. 3. 101

[2387]   Lay thy head in Furies' lap.

5. 3. 103

[2388]   Let vultures vile seize on his lungs.

5. 3. 135

[2389]   Thou damned tripe-visaged rascal.

5. 4. 9

[2390]   Thou paper-faced villain.

5. 4. 11

[2391]   You thin man in a censer.

5. 4. 19

[2392]   You blue-bottle rogue.

5. 4. 20-21

[2393]   You filthy famished correctioner.

5. 4. 21

Thou atomy, thou! [2394]

5. 4. 29

I will leer upon him as he comes by. [2395]

5. 5. 6-7

[I am] hal'd thither by most mechanical and dirty hand. [2396]

5. 5. 35-36

How ill white hairs becomes a fool and jester! [2397]

5. 5. 48

Make less thy body hence, and more thy grace. [2398]

5. 5. 52

Leave gormandizing; the grave doth gape [2399]
For thee thrice wider than for other men.

5. 5. 53-54

Reply not to me with a fool-born jest. [2400]

5. 5. 55

[You were] the tutor and the feeder of my riots! [2401]

5. 5. 62

[You are] too much cloyed with fat meat. [2402]

Epi. 26-27

[He] shall die of a sweat, unless already he be killed with [2403]
your hard opinions.

Epi. 30-31

Henry V

[2404] His addiction was to courses vain;
His companies unletter'd, rude, and shallow;
His hours fill'd up with riots, banquets, sports;
And never noted in him any study,
Any retirement, any sequestration
From open haunts and popularity.

1. 1. 54-59

[2405] This mock of his hath turn'd his balls to gun-stones.

1. 2. 281-82

[2406] His jest will savour but of shallow wit
When thousands weep more than did laugh at it.

1. 2. 295-96

[2407] I have an humour to knock you indifferently well.

2. 1. 54

[2408] An oath of mickle might!

2. 1. 66

[2409] I thee defy again.

2. 1. 72

Put thy face between his sheets and do the office of a   [2410]
warming-pan.

> 2. 1. 83-84

He'll yield the crow a pudding one of these days.   [2411]

> 2. 1. 87-88

Base is the slave that pays!   [2412]

> 2. 1. 96

How smooth and even they do bear themselves!   [2413]
As if allegiance in their bosoms sat.

> 2. 2. 3-4

Thou cruel, ingrateful, savage and inhuman creature!   [2414]

> 2. 2. 94-95

> Tis so strange   [2415]
That, though the truth of it stands off as gross
As black and white, my eye will scarcely see it.

> 2. 2. 102-4

[You are] two yoke-devils sworn to either's purpose.   [2416]

> 2. 2. 106

> Whatsoever cunning fiend it was   [2417]
That wrought upon thee so preposterously
Hath got the voice in hell for excellence.

> 2. 2. 111-13

> Thy fall hath left a kind of blot,   [2418]
To mark the full-fraught man and best indued
With some suspicion.

> 2. 2. 138-40

[2419]   This revolt of thine, methinks, is like
Another fall of man.

2. 2. 141-42

[2420] They were devils incarnate.

2. 3. 32-33

[2421] [He] saw a flea stick upon [your] nose, and said it was a
black soul burning in hell.

2. 3. 41-43

[2422] Trust none; for oaths are straws, men's faiths are wafer-
cakes.

2. 3. 51-52

[2423] [You] vain, giddy, shallow, humorous youth!

2. 4. 28

[2424]   Coward dogs
Most spend their mouths when what they seem to
          threaten
Runs far before them.

2. 4. 69-71

[2425] Scorn and defiance; slight regard, comtempt,
And any thing that may not misbecome
The mighty sender, doth he prize you at.

2. 4. 117-19

[2426] I desire nothing but odds [with you].

2. 4. 128-29

[2427] [Your] chin is but enrich'd with one appearing hair.

3. Chorus. 22-23

[2428] Avaunt, you cullions!

3. 2. 21

Three such antics do not amount to a man.   [2429]

3. 2. 31-32

[You are] white-livered and red-faced.   [2430]

3. 2. 33

He hath a killing tongue and a quiet sword; by the means   [2431]
whereof he breaks words, and keeps whole weapons.

3. 2. 35-37

He hath heard that men of few words are the best men;   [2432]
and therefore he scorns to say his prayers, lest he should
be thought a coward.

3. 2. 37-40

His few bad words are matched with as few good deeds.   [2433]

3. 2. 40-41

He never broke any man's head but his own, and that   [2434]
was against a post when he was drunk.

3. 2. 42-43

[You] will steal any thing and call it purchase.   [2435]

3. 2. 44

[You] are sworn brothers in filching.   [2436]

3. 2. 47

[Your] villainy goes against my weak stomach, and there-   [2437]
fore I must cast it up.

3. 2. 55-57

He is an ass, as in the world: I will verify as much in his   [2438]
beard.

3. 2. 74-75

[2439] He has no more directions than is a puppy-dog. [sic]

3. 2. 75-77

[2440] I do not know you so good a man as myself: so Chrish save me, I will cut off your head. [sic]

3. 2. 135-36

[2441] Buy a slobbery and a dirty farm
In that nook-shotten isle.

3. 5. 13-14

[2442] [Your] madams mock at [you], and plainly say
[Your] mettle is bred out.

3. 5. 28-29

[2443] He'll drop his heart into the sink of fear.

3. 5. 59

[2444] Let hemp his wind-pipe suffocate.

3. 6. 44

[2445] Die and be damn'd! and figo for thy friendship!

3. 6. 58

[2446] The fig of Spain!

3. 6. 60

[2447] 'Tis a gull, a fool, a rogue, that now and then goes to the wars to grace himself at his return under the form of soldier.

3. 6. 68-70

[2448] What a beard of the general's cut and a horrid suit of the camp will do among foaming bottles and ale-washed wits, is wonderful to be thought on.

3. 6. 78-81

Such slanders of the age!   [2449]

                                    3. 6. 82

He is not the man that he would gladly make show to the   [2450]
world he is.

                                    3. 6. 84-86

His face is all bubukles, and whelks, and knobs, and   [2451]
flames o' fire; and his lips blows at his nose, and it is like
a coal of fire, sometimes plue, and sometimes red; but his
nose is executed, and his fire's out [sic].

                                    3. 6. 105-10

We would have all such offenders so cut off.   [2452]

                                    3. 6. 111

To this add defiance.   [2453]

                                    3. 6. 139

They that ride so, and ride not warily, fall into foul bogs. [2454]

                                    3. 7. 57-58

I could make as true a boast as that if I had a sow to my   [2455]
mistress.

                                    3. 7. 63-64

Your horse would trot as well were some of your brags   [2456]
dismounted.

                                    3. 7. 79-80

What a wretched and peevish fellow is he, to mope with   [2457]
his fat-brained followers so far out of his knowledge!

                                    3. 7. 133-35

If [they] had any apprehension, they would run away.   [2458]

                                    3. 7. 136-37

[2459] If their heads had any intellectual armour, they could never wear such heavy head-pieces.

3. 7. 138-40

[2460] Foolish curs! that run winking into the mouth of a Russian bear and have their heads crushed like rotten apples.

3. 7. 143-44

[2461] You may as well say that's a valiant flea that dare eat his breakfast on the lip of a lion.

3. 7. 145-46

[2462] The men do sympathize with the mastiffs in robustious and rough coming on, leaving their wits with their wives.

3. 7. 147-49

[2463]   Art thou an officer?
Or art thou base, common and popular?

4. 1. 37-38

[2464] I'll knock his leek about his pate.

4. 1. 54

[2465] Do not you wear your dagger in your cap, lest he knock that about [your pate].

4. 1. 56-57

[2466] The figo for thee then!

4. 1. 60

[2467] If the enemy is an ass and a fool and a prating coxcomb, is it meet, think you, that we should also, look you, be an ass and a fool and a prating coxcomb?

4. 1. 77-80

Though they can outstrip men, they have no wings to fly   [2468]
from God.

4. 1. 173-74

That's a perilous shot out of an elder-gun.   [2469]

4. 1. 203-4

You may as well go about to turn the sun to ice with   [2470]
fanning in his face with a peacock's feather.

4. 1. 205-7

I should be angry with you if the time were convenient.   [2471]

4. 1. 209-10

Let it be a quarrel between us, if you live.   [2472]

4. 1. 211

By this hand, I will take thee a box on the ear.   [2473]

4. 1. 221-22

      [I am] subject to the breath   [2474]
Of every fool, whose sense no more can feel
But his own wringing!

4. 1. 240-42

      [You are] a wretched slave   [2475]
Who with a body fill'd, and vacant mind
Gets him to rest, cramm'd with distressful bread.

4. 1. 274-76

[He] in gross brain little wots.   [2476]

4. 1. 288

      Let us but blow on them,   [2477]
The vapour of our valour will o'erturn them.

4. 2. 23-24

[2478] Crouch down in fear, and yield.

4. 2. 37

[2479] [They] sit like fixed candlesticks.

4. 2. 45

[2480] We would not die in that man's company.

4. 3. 38

[2481] Gentlemen in England now a-bed
Shall think themselves accurs'd they were not here,
And hold their manhoods cheap.

4. 3. 64-66

[2482]   Though buried in your dunghills,
They shall be famed; for there the sun shall greet them,
And draw their honours reeking up to heaven,
Leaving their earthly parts to choke your clime,
The smell whereof shall breed a plague.

4. 3. 99-103

[2483] Thou damned and luxurious mountain goat.

4. 4. 19

[2484] I'll fer him, and firk him, and ferret him.

4. 4. 28-29

[2485] I did never know so full a voice issue from so empty a
heart: but the saying is true, "The empty vessel makes
the greatest sound."

4. 4. 69-71

[2486] Reproach and everlasting shame
Sits mocking in [your] plumes.

4. 5. 4-5

[You] do offend our sight. [2487]

4. 7. 61

He be as good a gentleman as the devil is. [2488]

4. 7. 141-42

His reputation is as arrant a villain and a Jack-sauce as [2489]
ever his black shoe trod upon God's ground.

4. 7. 144-46

What an arrant, rascally, beggarly, lousy knave it is. [2490]

4. 8. 35-36

Your shoes is not so good. [2491]

4. 8. 73

[You are] no better than a fellow of no merits. [2492]

5. 1. 7-8

Eat my leek. [2493]

5. 1. 9

Here he comes, swelling like a turkey-cock. [2494]

5. 1. 15-16

Art thou bedlam? [2495]

5. 1. 19

If you can mock a leek you can eat a leek. [2496]

5. 1. 38-39

By this leek, I will most horribly revenge. [2497]

5. 1. 68-69

If I owe you any thing I will pay you in cudgels. [2498]

5. 1. 67

[2499] You shall be a woodmonger, and buy nothing of me but cudgels.

5. 1. 68-69

[2500] Dare not avouch in your deeds any of your words.

5. 1. 76-77

[2501] I have seen you gleeking and galling.

5. 1. 77

[2502] [He is] something lean to cut-purse of quick hand.

5. 1. 90

[2503] The tongues of men are full of deceits.

5. 2. 117-18

[2504] [You] lay on like a butcher.

5. 2. 144

[2505] [You] sit like a jackanapes.

5. 2. 144-45

[2506] [Your] face is not worth sunburning.

5. 2. 150

[2507] [You] hang like a new-married wife about her husband's neck, hardly to be shook off.

5. 2. 185-88

[2508] Old age, that ill layer-up of beauty, can do no more spoil upon [your] face.

5. 2. 242-43

Henry VI, Part 1

They must be dieted like mules,   [2509]
And have their provender tied to their mouths.

1. 2. 10-11

Let's leave this town; for they are hare-brain'd slaves.   [2510]

1. 2. 37

Shall I be flouted thus by dunghill grooms?   [2511]

1. 3. 14

I will not answer thee with words, but blows.   [2512]

1. 3. 69

Scoffs and scorns and contumelious taunts!   [2513]

1. 4. 38

[You are] the scarecrow that affrights our children so.   [2514]

1. 4. 42

[I'll] make a quagmire of your mingled brains.   [2515]

1. 4. 108

[2516] I will chastise this high-minded strumpet.

1. 5. 12

[2517] [You] partakers of a little gain!

2. 1. 52

[2518] This is a child, a silly dwarf!
This weak and writhled shrimp!

2. 3. 21-22

[2519] Laughest thou, wretch? Thy mirth shall turn to moan.

2. 3. 43

[2520] What you see is but the smallest part
And least proportion of humanity.

2. 3. 51-52

[2521] [You] riddling merchant!

2. 3. 56

[2522] [You are] no wiser than a daw.

2. 4. 18

[2523] The truth appears so naked on my side
That any purblind eye may find it out.

2. 4. 20-21

[2524] I'll note you in my book of memory,
To scourge you for this apprehension.

2. 4. 101-2

[2525] Go forward and be chok'd with thy ambition!

2. 4. 112

[2526] Such is thy audacious wickedness,
Thy lewd, pestiferous, and dissentious pranks,

As very infants prattle of thy pride!

                      3. 1. 14-16

Thou art a most pernicious usurer,   [2527]
Froward by nature, enemy to peace.

                      3. 1. 17

[You are] lascivious, wanton, more than well beseems   [2528]
A man of thy profession and degree.

                      3. 1. 19-20

[You] viperous worm that gnaws the bowels!   [2529]

                      3. 1. 72-73

[I've been] disgraced by an inkhorn mate.   [2530]

                      3. 1. 99

[You] talk like the vulgar sort of market men   [2531]
That come to gather money for their corn.

                      3. 2. 4-5

That witch, that damned sorceress,   [2532]
Hath wrought this hellish mischief unawares.

                      3. 2. 38-39

Scoff on, vile fiend and shameless courtezan!   [2533]
I trust ere long to choke thee with thine own.

                      3. 2. 45-46

[You] hag of all despite!   [2534]

                      3. 2. 52

             This fact was infamous   [2535]
And ill-beseeming any common man.

                      4. 1. 30-31

[2536] Be quite degraded, like a hedge-born swain.

4. 1. 43

[2537] Stain to thy countrymen, thou hear'st thy doom!

4. 1. 45

[2538] Be packing!

4. 1. 46

[2539] Let him perceive how ill we brook his treason,
And what offence it is to flout his friends.

4. 1. 74-75

[2540] This fellow here, with envious carping tongue,
Upbraided me.

4. 1. 90-91

[2541] Good Lord, what madness rules in brainsick men.

4. 1. 111

[2542] Vexation almost stops my breath.

4. 3. 41

[2543] [You] ireful Bastard!

4. 6. 16

[2544] [You are] the pillage of a giglot wench.

4. 7. 41

[2545] Here is a silly-stately style indeed!

4. 7. 72

[2546] Oh, were mine eyeballs into bullets turn'd,
That I in rage might shoot them at your faces!

4. 7. 89-90

[You] stink and putrefy the air. [2547]

4. 7. 90

Stoop and bend thy knee. [2548]

5. 1. 61

Thy glory droopeth to the dust. [2549]

5. 3. 29

See how the ugly witch doth bend her brows, [2550]
As if, with Circe, she would change my shape!

5. 3. 34-35

Chang'd to a worser shape thou canst not be. [2551]

5. 3. 36

Tush, that's a wooden thing! [2552]

5. 3. 89

This argues what her kind of life hath been, [2553]
Wicked and vile.

5. 4. 15-16

           I would the milk [2554]
Thy mother gave thee when thou suck'dst her breast
Had been a little ratsbane for thy sake!

5. 4. 27-29

           She hath liv'd too long, [2555]
To fill the world with vicious qualities.

5. 4. 34-35

You are polluted with your lusts, [2556]
Stain'd with the guiltless blood of innocents,
Corrupt and tainted with a thousand vices.

5. 4. 43-45

Henry VI, Part 2

[2557] Shameful is this league!

1. 1. 97

[2558]   If I longer stay
We shall begin our ancient bickerings.

1. 1. 142-43

[2559] Grovel on thy face.

1. 2. 9

[2560] [You have a] base and humble mind.

1. 2. 62

[2561] [You] tedious stumbling-blocks!

1. 2. 64

[2562] Contemptuous base-born callet!

1. 3. 83

[2563] Could I come near your beauty with my nails
I'd set my ten commandments in your face.

1. 3. 141-42

[You] base dunghill villain, and mechanical! [2564]

1. 3. 193

Descend to darkness and the burning lake! [2565]

1. 4. 38

'Tis but a base ignoble mind [2566]
That mounts no higher than a bird can soar.

2. 1. 13-14

[You're] the lying'st knave in Christendom. [2567]

2. 1. 124-25

[You are] a sort of naughty persons, lewdly bent. [2568]

2. 1. 159

In sight of God and us, your guilt is great. [2569]

2. 3. 2

This knave's tongue begins to double. [2570]

2. 3. 89

[You are] a pointing stock to every idle rascal. [2571]

2. 4. 46-47

[You're] the hindmost man. [2572]

3. 1. 2

Small curs are not regarded when they grin. [2573]

3. 1. 18

Seems he a dove? His feathers are but borrow'd. [2574]

3. 1. 75

[His] red sparkling eyes blab his heart's malice. [2575]

3. 1. 154

[2576] [Your] railing is intolerable.

3. 1. 172

[2577] [You are] cold in great affairs.

3. 1. 224

[2578] You put sharp weapons in a madman's hands.

3. 1. 347

[2579] Upon thy eye-balls murderous Tyranny
Sits in grim majesty to fright the world.

3. 2. 48-49

[2580] Art thou, like the adder, waxen deaf?

3. 2. 75

[2581] Thy mother took into her blameful bed
Some stern untutor'd churl.

3. 2. 211-12

[2582] [You] pernicious blood-sucker of sleeping men!

3. 2. 225

[2583] Unworthy though thou art, I'll cope with thee.

3. 2. 229

[2584] How quaint an orator you are.

3. 2. 273

[2585] [You are] a sort of tinkers.

3. 2. 276

[2586] Would curses kill, as doth the mandrake's groan,
I would invent as bitter searching terms,
As curst, as harsh, and horrible to hear,
Deliver'd strongly through my fixed teeth,
With full as many signs of deadly hate,

As lean-fac'd Envy in her loathsome cave.

3. 2. 309-14

To die by thee were but to die in jest. [2587]

3. 2. 399

[You] obscure and lowly swain! [2588]

4. 1. 50

Base slave, thy words are blunt, and so art thou. [2589]

4. 1. 67

Thy lips shall sweep the ground. [2590]

4. 1. 74

Wedded be thou to the hags of hell. [2591]

4. 1. 78

[You] paltry, servile, abject drudges! [2592]

4. 1. 104

Small things make base men proud. [2593]

4. 1. 105

Drones suck not eagles' blood but rob bee hives. [2594]

4. 1. 108

It is impossible that I should die [2595]
By such a lowly vassal as thyself.

4. 1. 109-10

The first thing we do, let's kill all the lawyers. [2596]

4. 2. 73

Hang him with his pen and ink-horn about his neck. [2597]

4. 2. 103-4

[2598] [You] silken-coated slaves!

4. 2. 122

[2599] Will you credit this base drudge's words,
That speaks he knows not what?

4. 2. 144-45

[2600] He can speak French; and therefore he is a traitor.

4. 2. 159-60

[2601]   A ragged multitude
Of hinds and peasants, rude and merciless!

4. 4. 31-3

[2602] Rascal people, thirsting after prey.

4. 5. 50

[2603] [Your] breath stinks with eating toasted cheese.

4. 7. 10-11

[2604] I am the [broom] that must sweep the court clean of such
filth as thou art.

4. 7. 28-30

[2605] Thou hast most traitorously corrupted the youth of the
realm in erecting a grammar-school.

4. 7. 30-32

[2606] It will be prov'd to thy face that thou hast men about thee
that usually talk of a noun, and a verb, and such abominable words as no Christian ear can endure to hear.

4. 7. 36-39

[2607] Away with him! away with him! he speaks Latin.

4. 7. 55

You are all recreants and dastards, and delight to live in slavery. [2608]

4. 8. 28-29

Was ever feather so lightly blown to and fro as this multitude? [2609]

4. 8. 55-56

Hence will I drag thee headlong by the heels [2610]
Unto a dunghill, which shall be thy grave,
And there cut off thy most ungracious head.

4. 10. 79-81

That is too much presumption on thy part. [2611]

5. 1. 38

Heap of wrath, foul indigested lump, [2612]
As crooked in thy manners as thy shape!

5. 1. 157-58

Take heed, lest by your heat you burn yourselves. [2613]

5. 1. 160

Thou mad misleader of thy brain-sick son! [2614]

5. 1. 163

Wilt thou on thy death-bed play the ruffian, [2615]
And seek for sorrow with thy spectacles?

5. 1. 164-65

You'll surely sup in hell. [2616]

5. 1. 217

Henry VI, Part 3

[2617] Patience is for poltroons, such as he.

1. 1. 62

[2618] In [your] cold blood no spark of honour bides.

1. 1. 190

[2619] Be thou a prey.

1. 1. 191

[2620]   Make thy sepulchre,
And creep into it far before thy time.

1. 1. 243-44

[2621] Your oath is vain and frivolous.

1. 2. 27

[2622] But that I hate thee deadly,
I should lament thy miserable state.

1. 4. 84-85

[2623] I to make thee mad do mock thee thus.

1. 4. 90

How ill-beseeming is it in thy sex   [2624]
To triumph like an Amazonian trull
Upon their woes whom Fortune captivates!

                                       1. 4. 113-15

Thy face is vizard-like.   [2625]

                                       1. 4. 116

'Tis beauty that doth oft make women proud;   [2626]
But God he knows thy share thereof is small.
'Tis virtue that doth make them most admir'd;
The contrary doth make thee wonder'd at.
'Tis government that makes them seem divine;
The want thereof makes thee abominable.
Thou art as opposite to every good
As the Antipodes are unto us.

                                       1. 4. 128-35

O tiger's heart wrapp'd in a woman's hide!   [2627]

                                       1. 4. 137

In thy need such comfort come to thee   [2628]
As now I reap at thy too cruel hand!

                                       1. 4. 165-66

[You are] trimm'd like a younker prancing to his love!   [2629]

                                       2. 1. 24

Go rate thy minions, proud insulting boy!   [2630]

                                       2. 2. 84

Thou art neither like thy sire nor dam,   [2631]
But like a foul misshapen stigmatic,
Mark'd by the Destinies to be avoided,
As venom toads, or lizards' dreadful stings.

                                       2. 2. 135-38

[2632] [You] common people swarm like summer flies.

2. 6. 8

[2633] Commanded always by the greater gust,
Such is the lightness of you common men.

3. 1. 87-88

[2634] [You are] the bluntest wooer in Christendom.

3. 2. 83

[2635] [You are] impudent and shameless.

3. 3. 156

[2636] [You] feigned friend!

4. 2. 11

[2637] You are the fount that makes small brooks to flow.

4. 8. 54

[2638] Thou art no Atlas for so great a weight.

5. 1. 36

[2639] I had rather chop this hand off at a blow
And with the other fling it at thy face.

5. 1. 50-51

[2640] [You] bug!

5. 2. 2

[2641] [Thou] ruthless sea, [thou] quicksand of deceit, [thou]
ragged fatal rock!

5. 4. 25-27

[2642]   He might infect another
And make him of like spirit to himself.

5. 4. 46-47

Be mock'd and wonder'd at. [2643]

5. 4. 57

His currish riddles sorts not with this place. [2644]

5. 5. 26

For God's sake, take away this captive scold. [2645]

5. 5. 29

Untutor'd lad, thou art too malapert. [2646]

5. 5. 32

Thou misshapen Dick! [2647]

5. 5. 35

Why should she live to fill the world with words? [2648]

5. 5. 43

By heaven, I will not do thee so much ease. [2649]

5. 5. 70

A persecutor I am sure thou art. [2650]

5. 6. 31

The owl shriek'd at thy birth, an evil sign. [2651]

5. 6. 44

Thy mother felt more than a mother's pain, [2652]
And yet brought forth less than a mother's hope.

5. 6. 49-50

[You] indigest deformed lump! [2653]

5. 6. 51

Teeth hadst thou in thy head when thou wast born, [2654]
To signify thou cam'st to bite the world.

5. 6. 53-54

[2655] Down, down to hell; and say I sent thee thither.

5. 6. 67

[2656] Snarl, and bite, and play the dog.

5. 6. 77

[2657]   So Judas kiss'd his master
And cried 'All hail!' when as he meant all harm.

5. 7. 33-34

[2658] Farewell, sour annoy!

5. 7. 45

Henry VIII

No man's pie is freed from [your] ambitious finger. [2659]

1. 1. 52-53

Such a keech can with his very bulk [2660]
Take up the rays o'th'beneficial sun,
And keep it from the earth.

1. 1. 55-57

Spider like, out of his self-drawing web, [he] gives us [2661]
note.

1. 1. 63-64

I can see his pride peep through each part of him. [2662]

1. 1. 68-69

He begins a new hell in himself. [2663]

1. 1. 71-72

Lo, where comes that rock that I advise your shunning. [2664]

1. 1. 113-14

This butcher's cur is venom-mouth'd. [2665]

1. 1. 120

[2666] As he cried 'Thus let be,' to as much end as give a crutch to th'dead.

1. 1. 171-72

[2667] These exactions, they are most most pestilent to th'hearing.

1. 2. 47-49

[2668] I am traduc'd by ignorant tongues.

1. 2. 71-72

[2669] Malicious censurers, which ever
As rav'nous fishes, do a vessel follow,
That is new trimm'd, but benefit no further
Than vain longing.

1. 2. 78-81

[2670] He hath into monstrous habits put the graces that once were his.

1. 2. 121-23

[2671] [Your] will is most malignant.

1. 2. 141

[2672] There's mischief in this man.

1. 2. 187

[2673] When they hold 'em, you would swear directly their very noses had been counsellors, they keep state so.

1. 3. 8-10

[2674] They have all new legs, and lame ones.

1. 3. 11

[2675] Their clothes are after such a pagan cut to't
That sure th'have worn out Christendom.

1. 3. 14-15

The sly whoresons have got a speeding trick to lay down ladies.

[2676]

> 1. 3. 39-40

The devil fiddle 'em, I am glad they are going.

[2677]

> 1. 3. 42

I am richer than my base accusers that never knew what truth meant.

[2678]

> 2. 1. 104-5

His conscience has crept too near another lady.

[2679]

> 2. 2. 7-18

For living murmurers there's places of rebuke.

[2680]

> 2. 2. 130-31

A very fresh fish here!

[2681]

> 2. 3. 86

I do believe [induc'd by potent circumstances] that you are mine enemy.

[2682]

> 2. 4. 73-75

[Thou art] not at all a friend to truth.

[2083]

> 2. 4. 81-82

Your heart is cramm'd with arrogancy, spleen and pride.

[2684]

> 2. 4. 107-8

I abhor this dilatory sloth.

[2685]

> 2. 4. 234-35

They should be good men, their affairs as righteous:
But all hoods make not monks.

[2686]

> 3. 1. 22-23

[2687] Woe upon ye, and all such false professors!

3. 1. 114-15

[2688] He appears as I would wish mine enemy.

3. 2. 27-28

[2689] Some strange commotion is in [your] brain.

3. 2. 112-13

[2690] In most strange postures we have seen him set himself.

3. 2. 118-19

[2691] Better have burnt that tongue than said so.

3. 2. 253-54

[2692] You have as little honesty as honour.

3. 2. 271

[2693] Can [I] endure to hear this arrogance? And from this fellow?

3. 2. 278-79

[2694] If we live thus tamely, to be thus jaded by a piece of scarlet, farewell nobility!

3. 2. 279-81

[2695] All goodness is poison to thy stomach.

3. 2. 282-83

[2696] How much methinks, I could despise this man.

3. 2. 297

[2697] Speak on sir, I dare your worst objections: if I blush, it is to see a nobleman want manners.

3. 2. 306-8

He was a man of an unbounded stomach. [2698]

4. 2. 33-34

He's a rank weed, and we must root him out. [2699]

5. 1. 52-53

You are potently oppos'd, and with a malice of as great [2700]
size.

5. 1. 134-35

You take a precipice for no leap of danger, and woo your [2701]
own destruction.

5. 1. 139-40

This is a piece of malice. [2702]

5. 2. 7

Your painted gloss discovers to men that understand you, [2703]
words and weakness.

5. 2. 105-6

You are strangely troublesome. [2704]

5. 2. 128

Ye blew the fire that burns ye: now have at ye. [2705]

5. 2. 147

Ye were ever good at sudden condemnations. [2706]

5. 2. 156

To me you cannot reach. You play the spaniel, [2707]
And think with wagging of your tongue to win me.

5. 2. 160-61

Wait like a lousy footboy. [2708]

5. 2. 174

[2709] Ye rude slaves, leave your gaping.

5. 3. 2-3

[2710] Bless me, what a fry of fornication is at door!

5. 3. 34-35

[2711] He should be a brazier by his face, for o'my conscience twenty of the dog-days now reign in's nose; all that stand about him are under the line, they need no other penance.

5. 3. 39-42

[2712] Three times was his nose discharg'd against me; he stands there like a mortar-piece to blow us.

5. 3. 43-45

[2713] Wife of small wit!

5. 3. 46

[2714] Faithful friends o'th'suburbs!

5. 3. 71

[2715] Y'are lazy knaves, and here ye lie baiting of bombards when ye should do service.

5. 3. 79-81

Julius Caesar

You blocks, you stones, you worse than senseless things! [2716]

1. 1. 35

He is a dreamer. Let us leave him. [2717]

1. 2. 24

His coward lips did from their colour fly. [2718]

1. 2. 121

[You] fat, sleek-headed men! [2719]

1. 2. 189-90

He thinks too much: such men are dangerous. [2720]

1. 2. 192

I can as well be hang'd as tell the manner of it: it was [2721]
mere foolery.

1. 2. 231-32

The rabblement hooted, and clapp'd their chapped [2722]
hands, and threw up their sweaty night-caps, and

uttered such a deal of stinking breath that it had, almost, choked [us].

1. 2. 240-44

[2723] I durst not laugh, for fear of opening my lips and receiving the bad air [from your stinking breath].

1. 2. 246-47

[2724] What a blunt fellow is this grown to be!

1. 2. 292

[2725] What rubbish and what offal!

1. 3. 109

[2726] [You] fleering tell-tale!

1. 3. 117

[2727] Think him as a serpent's egg, which, hatch'd, would, as his kind, grow mischievious.

2. 1. 32-33

[2728] Where wilt thou find a cavern dark enough to mask thy monstrous visage?

2. 1. 79-81

[2729] Every man hence to his idle bed.

2. 1. 117

[2730] He is given to sports, to wildness, and much company.

2. 1. 188-89

[2731] When I tell him he hates flatterers, he says he does, being then most flattered.

2. 1. 207-8

[2732] You have some sick offence within your mind.

2. 1. 268

Dwell I but in the suburbs of your good pleasure? [2733]
2. 1. 285-86

[You have] that which melteth fools—I mean sweet words, [2734]
low-crooked curtsies, and base spaniel fawning.
3. 1. 42-43

I spurn thee like a cur out of my way. [2735]
3. 1. 46

Your purpled hands do reek and smoke. [2736]
3. 1. 158

[You are] a slight unmeritable man, meet to be sent on [2737]
errands.
4. 1. 12-13

Though we lay these honours on this man, he shall but [2738]
bear them as the ass bears gold.
4. 1. 19-21

He's a tried and valiant soldier. [2739]
So is my horse.
4. 1. 28-29

He must be taught, and train'd, and bid go forth: a [2740]
barren-spirited fellow.
4. 1. 35-36

Do not talk of him but as a property. [2741]
4. 1. 39-40

I had rather be a dog, and bay the moon, than such a [2742]
one.
4. 3. 27-28

[2743] Have mind upon your health; tempt me no farther.

4. 3. 36

[2744] Must I give way and room to your rash choler? Shall I be frighted when a madman stares?

4. 3. 40

[2745] Fret till your proud heart break.

4. 3. 42

[2746] I'll use you for my mirth, yea, for my laughter,
When you are waspish.

4. 3. 49-50

[2747] There is no terror in your threats;
For I am arm'd so strong in honesty
That they pass by me as the idle wind,
Which I respect not.

4. 3. 66-69

[2748] I do not like your faults.

4. 3. 88

[2749] How vilely doth this cynic rhyme!

4. 3. 132

[2750] You show'd your teeth like apes, and fawn'd like hounds, and bow'd like bondmen.

5. 1. 41-42

[2751] I do find it cowardly and vile.

5. 1. 104

[2752] I perceive but cold demeanor.

5. 2. 3-4

King John

Be thou the sullen presage of your own decay.   [2753]

1. 1. 27-28

It must go wrong with you and me.   [2754]

1. 1. 41

        On my knee   [2755]
I give heaven thanks I was not like to thee!

1. 1. 82-83

What a madcap hath heaven lent us here!   [2756]

1. 1. 84

He hath a half-face.   [2757]

1. 1. 92

[He has] legs [like] riding-rods, arms [like] eel-skins   [2758]
stuff'd.

1. 1. 140-41

Sell your face for five pence and 'tis dear.   [2759]

1. 1. 153

[2760] If his name be George, I'll call him Peter.

1. 1. 186

[2761]   Where is he, that slave,
That holds in chase mine honour up and down?

1. 1. 222-23

[2762] We coldly pause for thee.

2. 1. 53

[2763] [You] rash, inconsiderate, firey voluntaries,
With ladies' faces and fierce dragons' spleens!

2. 1. 67-68

[2764] You are the hare of whom the proverb goes,
Whose valour plucks dead lions by the beard.

2. 1. 137-38

[2765] I'll smoke your skin-coat.

2. 1. 139

[2766] What cracker is this same that deafs our ears
With this abundance of superfluous breath?

2. 1. 147-48

[2767] [I am] infortunate in nothing but in thee.

2. 1. 178

[2768] They shoot but calm words folded up in smoke,
To make a faithless error of your ears.

2. 1. 229-30

[2769] I would set an ox-head to your lion's hide,
And make a monster of you.

2. 1. 292-93

Now he feasts, mousing the flesh of men. [2770]

2. 1. 354

Leave them as naked as the vulgar air. [2771]

2. 1. 387

Here's a large mouth indeed, [2772]
That spits forth death and mountains, rocks and seas,
Talks as familiarly of roaring lions
As maids of thirteen do of puppy-dogs!

2. 1. 457-60

He speaks plain cannon, fire, and smoke, and bounce; [2773]
He gives the bastinado with his tongue.

2. 1. 462-63

Zounds! I was never so bethump'd with words [2774]
Since I first call'd my brother's father dad.

2. 1. 466-67

[He is] drawn in the flattering table of her eye! [2775]
Hang'd in the frowning wrinkle of her brow!
And quarter'd in her heart!

2. 1. 504-6

So vile a lout! [2776]

2. 1. 509

That same purpose-changer, that sly divel, that broker, [2777]
that still breaks the pate of faith, that daily break-vow!

2. 1. 567-69

This bawd, this broker, this all-changing word! [2778]

2. 1. 582

[2779]
Thy word
Is but the vain breath of a common man.

2. 2. 7-8

[2780] Believe me, I do not believe thee, man.

2. 2. 9

[2781] This news hath made thee a most ugly man.

2. 2. 37

[2782]
[Thou art] grim,
Ugly, and sland'rous to thy mother's womb,
Full of unpleasing blots and sightless stains,
Lame, foolish, crooked, swart, prodigious,
Patch'd with foul moles and eye-offending marks.

2. 2. 43-47

[2783] Thou little valiant, great in villainy!

3. 1. 42

[2784] Thou fortune's champion, that dost never fight
But when her humorous ladyship is by
To teach thee safety!

3. 1. 44-46

[2785]
What a fool art thou,
A ramping fool, to brag, and stamp, and swear.

3. 1. 47-48

[2786] Thou wear a lion's hide! doff it for shame,
And hang a calve's-skin on those recreant limbs.

3. 1. 54-55

[2787]
[I] cannot devise a name
So slight, unworthy and ridiculous.

3. 1. 75-76

These giddy loose suggestions! [2788]

3. 1. 218

Will not a calve's-skin stop that mouth of thine? [2789]

3. 1. 225

Thy rage shall burn thee up, and thou shalt turn to [2790]
ashes.

3. 1. 270-71

[You are] all too wanton and too full of gauds. [2791]

3. 2. 46

He is a very serpent in my way. [2792]

3. 2. 71

Look, who comes here! a grave unto a soul; [2793]
Holding th' eternal spirit, against her will,
In the viled prison of affected breath.

3. 3. 17-19

Thou odoriferous stench! sound rottenness! [2794]

3. 3. 26

How green you are and fresh in this old world! [2795]

3. 3. 145

Are you more stubborn-hard than hammer'd iron? [2796]

4. 1. 67

The image of a wicked heinous fault [2797]
Lives in [your] eye.

4. 2. 71-72

[You] lean unwash'd artificer! [2798]

4. 2. 201

[2799] Out, dunghill!

4. 3. 87

[2800] I am stifled with this smell of sin.

4. 3. 113

[2801] There is not yet so ugly a fiend of hell
As thou shalt be.

4. 3. 123-24

[2802] I do suspect thee very grievously.

4. 3. 134

[2803] [You] unhair'd sauciness!

5. 2. 133

[2804] Hug with swine!

5. 2. 142

[2805] We hold our time too precious to be spent
With such a brabbler.

5. 2. 161-62

[2806]   [You are] a resolved villain
Whose bowels suddenly burst out.

5. 6. 29-30

[2807] All this thou seest is but a clod and module.

5. 7. 57-58

King Lear

An admirable evasion of whoremaster man, to lay his [2808]
goatish disposition to the charge of a star!

1. 2. 133-34

Pat he comes, like the catastrophe of the old comedy. [2809]

1. 2. 141-42

You base foot-ball player! [2810]

1. 4. 91

That's a sheal'd peascod. [2811]

1. 4. 208

Blasts and fogs upon thee! [2812]

1. 4. 308

I have seen drunkards do more than this in sport. [2813]

2. 1. 35-36

[You are] a knave, a rascal, an eater of broken meats; a [2814]
base, proud, shallow, beggarly, three-suited, hundred-
pound, filthy worsted-stocking knave; a lily-livered,
action-taking, whoreson, glass-gazing, super-serviceable,

finical rogue; one-trunk-inheriting slave; one that wouldst be a bawd in way of good service, and art nothing but the composition of a knave, beggar, coward, pander, and the son and heir of a mongrel bitch: one whom I will beat into clamorous whining if thou deni'st the least syllable of thy addition.

2. 2. 13-23

[2815] What a brazen-fac'd varlet art thou.

2. 2. 27

[2816] You rogue! I'll make a sop o' th' moonshine of you. You whoreson cullionly barber-monger!

2. 2. 30-33

[2817] I'll carbonado your shanks.

2. 2. 38

[2818] You cowardly rascal, nature disclaims in thee: a tailor made thee.

2. 2. 55

[2819] A stone-cutter or a painter could not have made him so ill, though they had been but two years o' th' trade.

2. 2. 58-60

[2820] Thou whoreson zed! thou unnecessary letter!

2. 2. 64

[2821] I will tread this unbolted villain into mortar, and daub the wall of a jakes with him.

2. 2. 65-67

[2822] I have seen better faces in my time
Than stands on any shoulder that I see
Before me at this instant.

2. 2. 94-96

These kind of knaves I know, which in this plainness   [2823]
Harbour more craft and more corrupter ends
Than twenty silly-ducking observants,
That stretch their duties nicely.

                              2. 2. 102-5

Ha! Mak'st thou this shame thy pastime?   [2824]

                              2. 4. 5-6

Ha, ha! he wears cruel garters.   [2825]

                              2. 4. 7

All the stor'd vengeances of Heaven fall   [2826]
On her ingrateful top! Strike her young bones,
You taking airs, with lameness!
You nimble lightnings, dart your blinding flames
Into her scornful eyes! Infect her beauty,
You fen-suck'd fogs, drawn by the pow'rful sun,
To fall and blister her!

                              2. 4. 163-69

This is a slave, whose easy-borrow'd pride   [2827]
Dwells in the fickle grace of her he follows.
Out, varlet, from my sight!

                              2. 4. 187-89

Thou art a boil, a plague-sore, or embossed carbuncle, in   [2828]
my corrupted blood.

                              2. 4. 225-27

Here's grace and a cod-piece; that's a wise man and a   [2829]
fool.

                              3. 2. 40-41

Now all the plagues that in the pendulous air hang fated   [2830]
o'er men's faults light on thy daughters!

                              3. 4. 67-68

[2831] [You are] false of heart, light of ear, bloody of hand; hog in sloth, fox in stealth, wolf in greediness, dog in madness, lion in prey.

3. 4. 93-95

[2832] Unaccommodated man is no more but such a poor, bare, forked animal as thou art.

3. 4. 109-11

[2833] This is the foul Flibbertigibbet.

3. 4. 118

[2834] He's mad that trusts in the tameness of a wolf, a horse's health, a boy's love, or a whore's oath.

3. 6. 18-19

[2835] Throw this slave upon the dunghill.

3. 7. 95-96

[2836] You are not worth the dust which the rude wind blows in your face.

4. 2. 30-31

[2837] Filths savour but themselves.

4. 2. 39

[2838] [You are] a moral fool.

4. 2. 58

[2839] See thyself, devil! Proper deformity shows not in the fiend so horrid as in woman.

4. 2. 59-61

[2840] Marry, your manhood-mew!

4. 2. 68

O thou side-piercing sight!   [2841]

4. 6. 85

Get thee glass eyes; and, like a scurvy politician, seem to   [2842]
see the things thou dost not.

4. 6. 172-74

I shall try whether your costard or my ballow [cudgel] be   [2843]
the harder.

4. 6. 242-43

Out, dunghill!   [2844]

4. 6. 245

Chill pick your teeth.   [2845]

4. 6. 246

A serviceable villain; as duteous to the vices of thy mis-   [2846]
tress as badness would desire.

4. 6. 254-56

[You] gilded butterflies!   [2847]

5. 3. 13

From th' extremest upward of thy head   [2848]
To the descent and dust below thy foot,
A most toad-spotted traitor.

5. 3. 136-38

With the hell-hated lie o'erwhelm thy heart.   [2849]

5. 3. 147

Love's Labour's Lost

[2850]   Fat paunches have lean pates.

                                    1. 1. 26

[2851]   [You are] like an envious sneaping frost
         That bites the first-born infants of the spring.

                                    1. 1. 100-1

[2852]   The music of his own vain tongue
         Doth ravish [him] like enchanting harmony.

                                    1. 1. 165-66

[2853]   There's villany abroad.

                                    1. 1. 186-87

[2854]   [He is] that low-spirited swain, that base minnow of thy
         mirth.

                                    1. 1. 240-41

[2855]   [You] unlettered small-knowing soul.

                                    1. 1. 243

[2856]   I will praise an eel with the same praise.

                                    1. 2. 26

I am ill at reckoning; it fitteth the spirit of a tapster. [2857]

1. 2. 39

Define, define, well-educated infant. [2858]

1. 2. 89

Such short-liv'd wits do wither as they grow. [2859]

2. 1. 54

Your wit's too hot, it speeds too fast, 'twill tire. [2860]

2. 1. 120

A horse to be ambassador for an ass! [2861]

3. 1. 49-50

Sweet smoke of rhetoric! [2862]
I shoot thee at the swain.

3. 1. 60-62

A most acute juvenal; voluble and free of grace! [2863]
By thy favour, sweet welkin, I must sigh in thy face.

3. 1. 64-65

I smell some l'envoy, some goose in this. [2864]

3. 1. 119-20

Regent of love rhymes, lord of folded arms, [2865]
The anointed sovereign of sighs and groans
Liege of all loiterers and malcontents,
Dread prince of plackets, king of codpieces,
Sole imperator and great general
Of trotting paritors: O my little heart!

3. 1. 178-83

A woman that is like a German clock, [2866]
Still a-repairing, ever out of frame,
And never going aright, being a watch,

But being watch'd that it may still go right!

> 3. 1. 187-90

[2867] [You are] a whitely wanton with a velvet brow,
With two pitch-balls stuck in [your] face for eyes.

> 3. 1. 193-94

[2868] [You] pernicious and indubitate beggar!

> 4. 1. 67

[2869] Come, come, you talk greasily; your lips grow foul.

> 4. 1. 136

[2870] By my soul, a swain! a most simple clown!

> 4. 1. 139

[2871]   Most incony vulgar wit;
When it comes so smoothly off, so obscenely as it were,
        so fit.

> 4. 1. 141-42

[2872] Most barbarous intimation!

> 4. 2. 13

[2873] [You have an] undressed, unpolished, uneducated,
unpruned, untrained, or rather unlettered, or ratherest,
unconfirmed fashion.

> 4. 2. 16-19

[2874] O! thou monster Ignorance, how deform'd dost thou look.

> 4. 2. 23

[2875] He hath never fed of the dainties that are bred in a book.
He hath not eat paper, as it were; he hath not drunk ink:
his intellect is not replenished; he is only an animal, only
sensible in the duller parts.

> 4. 2. 24-27

Perge, perge; so it shall please you to abrogate scurrility. [2876]

4. 2. 52-53

[You are] a foolish extravagant spirit, fool of forms, fig- [2877]
ures, shapes, objects, ideas, apprehensions, motions,
revolutions.

4. 2. 66-68

[This is] he that is likest to a hogshead. [2878]

4. 2. 85

[You are] a good lustre of conceit in a turf of earth. [2879]

4. 2. 86-87

[Here's] fire enough for a flint, pearl enough for a swine. [2880]

4. 2. 87-88

[You're] for smelling out the odiferous flowers of fancy, [2881]
the jerks of invention.

4. 2. 125-26

          Stoop, I say;
[Your] shoulder is with child. [2882]

4. 3. 87-88

Now step I forth to whip hypocrisy. [2883]

4. 3. 149

What grace hast thou, thus to reprove these worms? [2884]

4. 3. 151-52

O, what a scene of foolery have I seen! [2885]

4. 3. 161

O! me with what strict patience have I sat, [2886]
To see a king transformed to a gnat;
To see great Hercules whipping a gig,

And profound Solomon to tune a jig,
And Nestor play at push-pin with the boys,
And critic Timon laugh at idle toys!

4. 3. 163-68

[2887] Ah! you whoreson loggerhead, you were born to do me shame.

4. 3. 202

[2888] Will these turtles be gone?

4. 3. 209

[2889] I never knew man hold vile stuff so dear.

4. 3. 273

[2890] Barren practisers!

4. 3. 322

[2891] His humour is lofty, his discourse peremptory, his tongue filed, his eye ambitious, his gait majestical, and his general behaviour vain, ridiculous, and thrasonical. He is too picked, too spruce, too affected, too odd, as it were, too peregrinate, as I may call it.

5. 1. 10-15

[2892] He draweth out the thread of his verbosity finer than the staple of his argument.

5. 1. 17-18

[2893] I abhor such fanatical phantasimes, such insociable and point-devise companions; such rackers of orthography.

5. 1. 18-20

[2894] They have been at a great feast of languages, and stolen the scraps.

5. 1. 37-38

I marvel [he] hath not eaten thee for a word;
Thou art easier swallowed than a flapdragon.

[2895]

> 5. 1. 40-43

Thou disputes like an infant: go, whip thy gig.

[2896]

> 5. 1. 63

I will whip about your infamy.

[2897]

> 5. 1. 64-65

Thou half-penny purse of wit, thou pigeon-egg of discretion.

[2898]

> 5. 1. 69-70

Go to; thou hast it 'ad dunghill', at the fingers' ends, as they say.

[2899]

> 5. 1. 73-74

O, I smell false Latin.

[2900]

> 5. 1. 75

We will be singled from the barbarous.

[2901]

> 5. 1. 77

It will please his grace, by the world, sometime to lean
upon my poor shoulder, and with his royal finger, thus,
to dally with my excrement.

[2902]

> 5. 1. 96-99

He is not quantity enough for that Worthy's thumb: he is
not so big as the end of [Hercules'] club.

[2903]

> 5. 1. 126-28

He hath been five thousand year a boy.

[2904]

> 5. 2. 11

[2905] What's your dark meaning, mouse, of this light word?

5. 2. 19

[2906] A pox of that jest! and I beshrew all shrews!

5. 2. 46

[2907] [You are] a huge translation of hypocrisy,
Vilely compil'd, profound simplicity.

5. 2. 51-52

[2908] Look, how you butt yourself in these sharp mocks.

5. 2. 251

[2909] The tongues of mocking wenches are as keen
As is the razor's edge invisible,
Cutting a smaller hair than may be seen;
Above the sense of sense; so sensible
Seemeth their conference; their conceits have wings
Fleeter than arrows, bullets, wind, thought, swifter
things.

5. 2. 256-61

[2910] By heaven, [you are] all dry-beaten with pure scoff!

5. 2. 263

[2911] Are these the breed of wits so wonder'd at?

5. 2. 266

[2912] Tapers they are, with your sweet breaths puff'd out.

5. 2. 267

[2913] Well-liking wits they have; gross, gross; fat, fat.

5. 2. 268

[2914] This fellow pecks up wit, as pigeons pease,
And utters it again when God doth please.

5. 2. 315-16

A blister on [your] sweet tongue!   [2915]

                                        5. 2. 335

Taffeta phrases, silken terms precise,   [2916]
Three-pil'd hyperboles, spruce affection,
Figures pedantical; these summer flies
Have blown me full of maggot ostentation.

                                        5. 2. 406-9

[This is] some carry-tale, some please-man, some slight   [2917]
        zany,
Some mumble-news, some trencher-knight, some Dick,
That smiles his cheek in years.

                                        5. 2. 463-65

A foolish mild man; an honest man, look you, and soon   [2918]
dashed!

                                        5. 2. 574-75

[You have] the face of an old Roman coin, scarce seen.   [2919]

                                        5. 2. 606

This is not generous, not gentle, not humble.   [2920]

                                        5. 2. 621

                    The world's large tongue   [2921]
Proclaims you for a man replete with mocks;
Full of comparisons and wounding flouts,
Which you on all estates will execute
That lie within the mercy of your wit.

                                        5. 2. 832-36

Weed this wormwood from your fruitful brain.   [2922]

                                        5. 2. 837

Macbeth

[2923] The multiplying villainies of nature
Do swarm upon him.

1. 2. 11-12

[2924] [You] rump-fed ronyon!

1. 3. 6

[2925]   You should be women,
And yet your beards forbid me to interpret
That you are so.

1. 3. 45-47

[2926] [Your] horrid image doth unfix my hair.

1. 3. 135

[2927]   Nothing in his life
Became him like the leaving it.

1. 4. 7-8

[2928] Pall thee in the dunnest smoke of Hell.

1. 5. 51

Your face is as a book, where men [2929]
May read strange matters.

> 1. 5. 62-63

In swinish sleep their drenched natures lie. [2930]

> 1. 7. 68-69

False face must hide what the false heart doth know. [2931]

> 1. 7. 83

[This is] a false creation [2932]
Proceeding from the heat-oppressed brain.

> 2. 1. 38-39

This is a sorry sight. [2933]

> 2. 2. 20

You do unbend your noble strength, to think [2934]
So brainsickly of things.

> 2. 2. 44-45

Infirm of purpose! [2935]

> 2. 2. 51

Be not lost so poorly in your thoughts. [2936]

> 2. 2. 70-71

Here's an equivocator, that could swear in both the scales [2937]
against either scale.

> 2. 3. 9-10

Go the primrose way to th' everlasting bonfire. [2938]

> 2. 3. 20-21

Drink, Sir, is a great provoker of three things, nose- [2939]
painting, sleep, and urine. Lechery, it provokes, and
unprovokes: it provokes the desire, but it takes away the

performance. Therefore, much drink may be said to be an equivocator with lechery: it makes him, and it mars him; it sets him on, and it takes him off; it persuades him, and disheartens him; makes him stand to, and not stand to: in conclusion, equivocates him in a sleep, and, giving him the lie, leaves him.

2. 3. 26-37

[2940] Confusion now hath made his masterpiece!

2. 3. 67

[2941] Approach the chamber, and destroy your sight with a new Gorgon.

2. 3. 72-73

[2942] To show an unfelt sorrow is an office
Which the false man does easy.

2. 3. 136-37

[2943] Where we are, there's daggers in men's smiles.

2. 3. 139-40

[2944] 'Tis said, they eat each other.

2. 4. 18

[2945] [You] half a soul!

3. 1. 82

[2946] Ay, in the catalogue ye go for men;
As hounds, and greyhounds, mongrels, spaniels, curs,
Shoughs, water-rugs, and demi-wolves, are clept
All by the name of dogs.

3. 1. 91-94

[2947] [You are] i' th' worst rank of manhood.

3. 1. 102

Thou art the best o' th' cut-throats. [2948]

3. 4. 16

Never shake thy gory locks at me. [2949]

3. 4. 49-50

When all's done, you look but on a stool. [2950]

3. 4. 66-67

[You are] quite unmann'd in folly. [2951]

3. 4. 72

Thy bones are marrowless, thy blood is cold. [2952]

3. 4. 93

Thou hast no speculation in those eyes, [2953]
Which thou dost glare with.

3. 4. 94-95

How now, you secret, black, and midnight hags! [2954]

4. 1. 48

What, you egg! Young fry of treachery! [2955]

4. 2. 82-83

[Your] sole name blisters our tongues. [2956]

4. 3. 12

           I grant him bloody, [2957]
Luxurious, avaricious, false, deceitful,
Sudden, malicious, smacking of every sin
That has a name.

4. 3. 57-60

Fit to govern? No, not to live. [2958]

4. 3. 102-3

[2959] I would not have such a heart in my bosom, for the dignity of the whole body.

5. 1. 52-53

[2960] Those he commands move only in command,
Nothing in love.

5. 2. 19-20

[2961]   Now does he feel his title
Hang loose about him, like a giant's robe
Upon a dwarfish thief.

5. 2. 20-22

[2962] All that is within him does condemn itself for being there.

5. 2. 24-25

[2963] Go, prick thy face, and over-red thy fear,
Thou lily-liver'd boy.

5. 3. 14-15

[2964]   [This] is a tale
Told by an idiot, full of sound and fury,
Signifying nothing.

5. 5. 26-28

[2965] Thou call'st thyself a hotter name than any is in hell.

5. 7. 6-7

[2966] The devil himself could not pronounce a title
More hateful to mine ear.

5. 7. 8-9

[2967] Thou bloodier villain than terms can give thee out!

5. 8. 7-8

[2968] Live to be the show and gaze o' th' time.

5. 8. 24

Measure for Measure

I think thou never wast where grace was said. [2969]

1. 2. 18-19

Behold, behold, where Madam Mitigation comes! [2970]

1. 2. 41

I have purchased many diseases under her roof. [2971]

1. 2. 42-43

Thy bones are hollow; impiety has made a feast of thee. [2972]

1. 2. 52-53

But what's his offence? [2973]
Groping for trouts, in a peculiar river.

1. 2. 82-83

Thy head stands so tickle on thy shoulders, that a milk- [2974]
maid, if she be in love, may sigh it off.

1. 2. 161-63

Come, you are a tedious fool. To the purpose. [2975]

2. 1. 115

[2976] Your bum is the greatest thing about you; so that, in the
beastliest sense, you are Pompey the Great.

2. 1. 214-16

[2977] You shall stifle in your own report,
And smell of calumny.

2. 4. 157-58

[2978]   Thou art not noble;
For all th'accommodations that thou bear'st
Are nurs'd by baseness.

3. 1. 13-15

[2979]   Thou'rt by no means valiant;
For thou dost fear the soft and tender fork
Of a poor worm.

3. 1. 15-17

[2980]   Thou hast nor youth, nor age,
But as it were an after-dinner's sleep
Dreaming on both.

3. 1. 32-33

[2981] Thou hast neither heat, affection, limb, nor beauty
To make thy riches pleasant.

3. 1. 37-38

[2982]   This outward-sainted deputy,
Whose settl'd visage and deliberate word
Nips youth i' th'head and follies doth enew
As falcon doth the fowl, is yet a devil:
His filth within being cast, he would appear
A pond as deep as hell.

3. 1. 88-93

[2983] I'll pray a thousand prayers for thy death;

No word to save thee.

3. 1. 145-46

Thy sin's not accidental, but a trade.   [2984]

3. 1. 148

Mercy to thee would prove itself a bawd;   [2985]
'Tis best that thou diest quickly.

3. 1. 149-50

Canst thou believe thy living is a life,   [2986]
So stinkingly depending? Go mend, go mend.

3. 2. 25 26

She hath eaten up all her beef, and she is herself in the   [2987]
tub.

3. 2. 54-55

Bawd is he doubtless, and of antiquity, too; bawd born.   [2988]

3. 2. 65-66

Go to kennel.   [2989]

3. 2. 82

He was begot between two stockfishes.   [2990]

3. 2. 105

It is certain that when he makes water, his urine is   [2991]
congealed ice.

3. 2. 105-7

For the rebellion of a codpiece!   [2992]
His use was to put a ducat in her clack-dish.

3. 2. 110-12

[You are] a very superficial, ignorant, unweighing fellow.   [2993]

3. 2. 123

[2994] You speak unskilfully: or, if your knowledge be more, it is much darkened in your malice.

3. 2. 142-44

[2995] He would mouth with a beggar though she smelt brown bread and garlic.

3. 2. 176-78

[2996] [You] have been an unlawful bawd time out of mind.

4. 2. 14-15

[2997] He's more, had I more name for badness.

5. 1. 61-62

[2998] That's somewhat madly spoken.

5. 1. 92

[2999] [You have] a blasting and a scandalous breath.

5. 1. 125

[3000] Silence that fellow! I would he had some cause to prattle for himself.

5. 1. 182-83

[3001] [You are] a fleshmonger, a fool, and a coward.

5. 1. 331-32

[3002] Such a fellow is not to be talked withal.

5. 1. 342

[3003] Away with those giglets!

5. 1. 345

[3004] Show your sheep-biting face, and be hanged an hour!

5. 1. 353

[3005] Hast thou or word, or wit, or impudence,

That yet can do thee office?

5. 1. 362-63

[You arc] a fool, a coward, one all of luxury, an ass, a
madman.

[3006]

5. 1. 498-99

Do not recompense me in making me a cuckold.

[3007]

5. 1. 514-15

Marrying a punk is pressing to death, whipping, and
hanging.

[3008]

5. 1. 520-21

The Merchant of Venice

[3009] [You're] such a want-wit!

1. 1. 6

[3010] Your mind is tossing on the ocean.

1. 1. 8

[3011] There are a sort of men whose visages
Do cream and mantle like a standing pond.

1. 1. 88-89

[3012] [You] only are reputed wise for saying nothing.

1. 1. 96-97

[3013] Fish not with this melancholy bait
For this fool gudgeon, this opinion.

1. 1. 101-2

[3014]   Silence is only commendable
In a neat's tongue dried, and a maid not vendible.

1. 1. 111-12

[3015] [You] speak an infinite deal of nothing.

1. 1. 113

[Your] reasons are as two grains of wheat hid in two [3016] bushels of chaff: you shall seek all day ere you find them, and when you have them, they are not worth the search.

1. 1. 115-18

I am much afeared my lady his mother played false with [3017] a smith.

1. 2. 41-43

I had rather be married to a death's-head with a bone in [3018] his mouth.

1. 2. 49-50

God made him, and therefore let him pass for a man. [3019]

1. 2. 53

He is every man in no man. [3020]

1. 2. 57

He will fence with his own shadow. [3021]

1. 2. 58-59

He is a proper man's picture, but alas! who can converse [3022] with a dumb-show?

1. 2. 69-70

When he is best, he is a little worse than a man, and [3023] when he is worst he is little better than a beast.

1. 2. 83-85

I will do any thing ere I will be married to a sponge. [3024]

1. 2. 94-95

[You] villain with a smiling cheek! [3025]

1. 3. 95

[3026] A goodly apple rotten at the heart.

1. 3. 96

[3027] I like not fair terms, and a villain's mind.

1. 3. 175

[3028] Do I look like a cudgel or a hovel-post, a staff, or a prop?

2. 2. 65-66

[3029] Thou hast got more hair on thy chin, than my fill-horse has on his tail.

2. 2. 90-91

[3030] Give him a present? Give him a halter!

2. 2. 100-1

[3031] A gentle riddance,—draw the curtains, go.

2. 7. 78

[3032] [I] will not jump me with common spirits,
And rank me with the barbarous multitudes.

2. 9. 32-33

[3033] How much low peasantry!

2. 9. 46

[3034] What's here? the portrait of a blinking idiot,
Presenting me a schedule!

2. 9. 54-55

[3035] O, these deliberate fools!

2. 9. 80

[3036] I would she were as lying a gossip in that, as ever knapp'd ginger, or made her neighbours believe she wept for the death of her third husband.

3. 1. 8-10

[You are] a bankrupt, a prodigal, who dare scarce show
his head.

[3037]

3. 1. 39-40

[You] soft and dull-ey'd fool.

[3038]

3. 3. 14

It is the most impenetrable cur
That ever kept with men.

[3039]

3. 3. 18-19

I have within my mind
A thousand raw tricks of these bragging Jacks,
Which I will practise.

[3040]

3. 4. 76-78

How every fool can play upon the word!

[3041]

3. 5. 40

I think the best grace of wit will shortly turn into silence,
and discourse grow commendable in none only but
parrots.

[3042]

3. 5. 40-43

Goodly Lord, what a wit-snapper are you!

[3043]

3. 5. 45

Wilt thou show the whole wealth of thy wit in an instant?

[3044]

3. 5. 50-51

O dear discretion, how his words are suited!
The fool hath planted in his memory
An army of good words, and I do know
A many fools that stand in better place,
Garnish'd like him, that for a tricksy word
Defy the matter.

[3045]

3. 5. 59-64

[3046] [You are] a stony adversary, an inhuman wretch,
Uncapable of pity, void, and empty
From any dram of mercy.

4. 1. 4-6

[3047] [You are] brassy bosoms and rough hearts of flint
Never train'd to offices of tender courtesy.

4. 1. 31-33

[3048] Some men, when the bagpipe sings i' th'nose,
Cannot contain their urine.

4. 1. 49-50

[3049] For thy life let justice be accus'd.

4. 1. 129

[3050] Thou but offend'st thy lungs to speak so loud.

4. 1. 140

[3051] Repair thy wit good youth, or it will fall
To cureless ruin.

4. 1. 141-42

[3052] I never knew so young a body with so old a head.

4. 1. 160-61

[3053] Beg that thou may'st have leave to hang thyself.

4. 1. 360

[3054] [Your body is a] muddy vesture of decay.

5. 1. 64

[3055] The motions of his spirit are dull as night.

5. 1. 86

[3056] A kind of boy, a little scrubbed boy, a prating boy!

5. 1. 162-64

The Merry Wives of Windsor

You Banbury cheese!   [3057]

1. 1. 118

[You] latten bilbo!

1. 1. 146

Froth and scum, thou liest!   [3058]

1. 1. 148

I say the gentleman had drunk himself out of his five [3059]
sentences.

1. 1. 157-58

O base Hungarian wight, wilt thou the spigot wield?   [3060]

1. 3. 19-20

He was gotten in drink.   [3061]

1. 3. 21

I am glad I am so acquit of this tinder-box: his thefts were [3062]
too open; his filching was like an unskilful singer; he kept
not time.

1. 3. 23-25

[3063] Then did the sun on dunghill shine.

1. 3. 59

[3064] O, she did so course o'er my exteriors with such a greedy intention that the appetite of her eye did seem to scorch me up like a burning-glass!

1. 3. 61-63

[3065] Rogues, hence, avaunt, vanish like hailstones; go; Trudge; plod away i' th' hoof; seek shelter, pack!

1. 3. 77-78

[3066] Let vultures gripe thy guts!

1. 3. 81

[3067] Thou art the Mars of Malcontents!

1. 3. 98

[3068] His guts are made of puddings.

2. 1. 31

[3069] What tempest threw this whale, with so many tuns of oil in his belly, ashore?

2. 1. 61-63

[3070] How shall I be revenged on him? I think the best way were to entertain him with hope till the wicked fire of lust have melted him in his own grease.

2. 1. 63-66

[3071] I will find you twenty lascivious turtles ere one chaste man.

2. 1. 77-78

[3072] Let's consult together against this greasy knight.

2. 1. 104-5

I love not the humour of bread and cheese.   [3073]

> 2. 1. 132-33

Faith, thou hast some crochets in thy head.   [3074]

> 2. 1. 148

There is either liquor in his pate or money in his purse   [3075]
when he looks so merrily.

> 2. 1. 182-83

Reason, you rogue, reason: think'st thou I'll endanger my   [3076]
soul *gratis*?

> 2. 2. 14-15

Why, thou unconfinable baseness, it is as much as I can   [3077]
do to keep the terms of my honour precise. Yet you,
rogue, will ensconce your rags, your cat-a-mountain
looks, your red-lattice phrases, and your bold beating
oaths, under the shelter of your honour!

> 2. 2. 19-27

Hang him, mechanical salt-butter rogue! I will stare him   [3078]
out of his wits, I will awe him with my cudgel: it shall
hang like a meteor o'er the cuckold's horns. Thou shalt
know I will predominate over the peasant, and thou shalt
lie with his wife.

> 2. 2. 267-72

[He's] a knave, and I will aggravate his style.   [3079]

> 2. 2. 272

What a damned Epicurean rascal is this?   [3080]

> 2. 2. 276

[He] is an ass, a secure ass: he will trust his wife, he will [3081]
not be jealous.

> 2. 2. 289-90

[3082] I will rather trust a Fleming with my butter, Parson Hugh the Welshman with my cheese, an Irishman with my aqua-vitae bottle, or a thief to walk my ambling gelding, than my wife with herself.

2. 2. 290-94

[3083] King-Urinal

2. 3. 31

[3084] Monsieur Mock-water

2. 3. 53-54

[3085] I will knog his urinals about his knave's costard.

3. 1. 13-14

[3086] I will knog your urinal about your knave's cogscomb for missing your meetings and appointments.

3. 1. 81-82

[3087] This same scall, scurvy, cogging companion!

3. 1. 110-11

[3088] I will smite his noddles.

3. 1. 116

[3089] We'll use this unwholesome humidity, this gross watery pumpion; we'll teach him to know turtles from jays.

3. 3. 35-37

[3090] [You] lisping hawthorn-buds that come like women in men's apparel, and smell like Bucklersbury in simple time!

3. 3. 65-67

[3091] A lousy knave, to have his gibes and his mockeries!

3. 3. 224-25

I had rather be set quick i' th'earth,
And bowl'd to death with turnips!

[3092]

3. 4. 84-85

If I be served such another trick, I'll have my brains ta'en out and buttered, and give them to a dog for a New Year's gift.

[3093]

3. 5. 6-8

[You] mountain of mummy!

[3094]

3. 5. 17

I'll no pullet-sperm in my brewage.

[3095]

3. 5. 28

[This is] the rankest compound of villainous smell that ever offended nostril.

[3096]

3. 5. 82-84

Fate, ordaining he should be a cuckold, held his hand.

[3097]

3. 5. 95-96

'Oman, art thou lunatics?

[3098]

4. 1. 60

Heaven guide him to thy husband's cudgel; and the devil guide his cudgel afterwards!

[3099]

4. 2. 80-81

We cannot misuse him enough.

[3100]

4. 2. 93-94

Why, this is lunatics; this is mad as a mad dog.

[3101]

4. 2. 115

Well said, brazen-face!

[3102]

4. 2. 124

[3103] He shall die a flea's death.

4. 2. 138-39

[3104] You witch, you rag, you baggage, you polecat, you runnion!

4. 2. 170-172

[3105] I'll have the cudgel hallowed and hung o'er the altar; it hath done meritorious service.

4. 2. 191-92

[3106] What would'st thou have, boor? What, thick-skin? speak, breathe, discuss; brief, short, quick, snap.

4. 5. 1-2

[3107] I'll provide you a chain, and I'll do what I can to get you a pair of horns.

5. 1. 5-6

[3108] I think the devil will not have [you] damned, lest the oil that's in [you] should set hell on fire.

5. 5. 35-36

[3109] Vile worm, thou wast o'erlook'd even in thy birth.

5. 5. 84

[3110] [You] drove the grossness of the foppery into a received belief, in despite of the teeth of all rhyme and reason.

5. 5. 125-27

[3111] Have I laid my brain in the sun and dried it, that it wants matter to prevent so gross o'er-reaching as this? 'Tis time I were choked with a piece of toasted cheese.

5. 5. 136-40

Have I lived to stand at the taunt of one that makes [3112]
fritters of English?

> 5. 5. 143-44

This is enough to be the decay of lust and late-walking [3113]
through the realm.

> 5. 5. 144-45

What, a hodge-pudding? A bag of flax? [3114]
A puffed man?
Old, cold, withered, and of intolerable entrails?
And one that is as slanderous as Satan?
And as poor as Job?
And as wicked as his wife?

> 5. 5. 152-57

[He is] given to fornications, and to taverns, and sack, [3115]
and wine, and metheglins [strong mead], and to
drinkings, and swearings, and starings, pribbles and
prabbles.

> 5. 5. 158-61

She's a great lubberly boy. [3116]

> 5. 5. 184

A Midsummer Night's Dream

[3117]   [You are] ill met by moonlight.

2. 1. 60

[3118]   With thy brawls thou hast disturb'd our sport.

2. 1. 87

[3119]   The green corn hath rotted ere his youth attain'd a beard.

2. 1. 94-95

[3120]   I love thee not, therefore pursue me not.

2. 1. 188

[3121]   You hard-hearted adamant!

2. 1. 195

[3122]   Do I not in plainest truth
Tell you I do not, nor I cannot love you?

2. 1. 200-1

[3123]   Tempt not too much the hatred of my spirit;
For I am sick when I do look on thee.

2. 1. 211-12

You spotted snakes with double tongue!   [3124]

                                       2. 2. 9

[You] thorny hedgehogs, newts and blind-worms!   [3125]

                               2. 2. 10-11

Wake when some vile thing is near.   [3126]

                                2. 2. 33

I do repent the tedious minutes I with [you] have spent. [3127]

                           2. 2. 110-11

For, as a surfeit of the sweetest things   [3128]
The deepest loathing to the stomach brings;
Or as the heresies that men do leave
Are hated most of those they did deceive;
So thou, my surfeit and my heresy,
Of all be hated, but the most of me!

                           3. 2. 136-41

What hempen homespuns have we swaggering here?   [3129]

                           3. 1. 73

What do you see? You see an ass-head of your own, do   [3130]
you?

                           3. 1. 111-12

I will purge thy mortal grossness so.   [3131]

                           3. 1. 153

[You] cowardly, giant-like ox-beef!   [3132]

                           3. 1. 185

My mistress with a monster is in love.   [3133]

                           3. 2. 6

[3134] A crew of patches, rude mechanicals, that work for bread!
3. 2. 9-10

[3135] [You're] the shallowest thick-skin of that barren sort.
3. 2. 13

[3136] [She] wak'd, and straightway lov'd an ass.
3. 2. 34

[3137] Henceforth be never number'd among men!
3. 2. 67

[3138] From thy hated presence part I so.
3. 2. 80

[3139] You do advance your cunning more and more.
3. 2. 128

[3140] If you were men, as men you are in show,
You would not use a gentle lady so.
3. 2. 151-52

[3141] Never did mockers waste more idle breath.
3. 2. 168

[3142] Thy threats have no more strength than her weak prayers.
3. 2. 250

[3143] Hang off, thou cat, thou burr! Vile thing, let loose,
Or I will shake thee from me like a serpent!
3. 2. 260-61

[3144] You juggler! You canker-blossom!
3. 2. 282

Have you no modesty, no maiden shame,   [3145]
No touch of bashfulness?

3. 2. 285-86

Thou painted maypole!   [3146]

3. 2. 296

How low am I? I am not yet so low   [3147]
But that my nails can reach unto thine eyes.

3. 2. 297-98

She was a vixen when she went to school,   [3148]
And though she be but little, she is fierce.

3. 2. 324-25

Get you gone, you dwarf;   [3149]
You minimus, of hindering knot-grass made;
You bead, you acorn.

3. 2. 328-30

[He's the] King of shadows.   [3150]

3. 2. 347

Methought I was enamour'd of an ass.   [3151]

4. 1. 76

O how mine eyes do loathe his visage now!   [3152]

4. 1. 78

Now when thou wak'st, with thine own fool's eyes peep.   [3153]

4. 1. 83

Lovers and madmen have such seething brains,   [3154]
Such shaping fantasies.

5. 1. 4-5

[3155] The lunatic, the lover, and the poet
Are of imagination all compact.

5. 1. 7-8

[3156] One sees more devils than vast hell can hold.

5. 1. 9

[3157] [They are] hard-handed men which never labour'd in
their minds till now.

5. 1. 72-73

[3158] He hath rid his prologue like a rough colt.

5. 1. 119

[3159] His speech was like a tangled chain; nothing impaired,
but all disordered.

5. 1. 124-25

[3160] One lion may [speak] when many asses do.

5. 1. 153

[3161] Would you desire lime and hair to speak better?

5. 1. 164

[3162] I kiss the wall's hole, not your lips at all.

5. 1. 199

[3163] This is the silliest stuff that ever I heard.

5. 1. 207

[3164] If we imagine no worse of them than they of themselves,
they may pass for excellent men.

5. 1. 211-12

[3165] This lion is a very fox for his valour and a goose for his
discretion.

5. 1. 224-25

He should have worn the horns on his head. [3166]

5. 1. 232

It appears by his small light of discretion that he is in the [3167]
wane.

5. 1. 243-44

Well moused, Lion! [3168]

5. 1. 258

With the help of a surgeon he might yet recover, and [3169]
prove an ass.

5. 1. 298-99

Much Ado About Nothing

[3170] He is no less than a stuffed man.

1. 1. 53

[3171] Four of his five wits went halting off, and now is the whole man governed with one.

1. 1. 59-61

[3172] If he have wit enough to keep himself warm, let him bear it for a difference between himself and his horse.

1. 1. 61-63

[3173] I see, lady, the gentleman is not in your books.
No; and he were, I would burn my study.

1. 1. 71-72

[3174] He will hang upon him like a disease.

1. 1. 78

[3175] He is sooner caught than the pestilence, and the taker runs presently mad.

1. 1. 78-80

I wonder that you will still be talking: nobody marks you.   [3176]
1. 1. 107-8

What, my dear Lady Disdain! Are you yet living?   [3177]
1. 1. 109

Courtesy itself must convert to disdain, if you come in   [3178]
her presence.
1. 1. 112-13

Truly I love none.   [3179]
A dear happiness to women, they would else have been
troubled with a pernicious suitor.
1. 1. 117-19

I had rather hear my dog bark at a crow than a man   [3180]
swear he loves me.
1. 1. 120-21

Scratching could not make [a face] worse, if 'twere   [3181]
such a face as yours were.
1. 1. 126 27

You are a rare parrot-teacher.   [3182]
A bird of my tongue is better than a beast of yours.
I would my horse had the speed of your tongue.
1. 1. 128-30

I noted her not, but I looked on her.   [3183]
1. 1. 152

She's too low for a high praise, too brown for a fair praise,   [3184]
and too little for a great praise.
1. 1. 159-61

Being no other but as she is, I do not like her.   [3185]
1. 1. 163-64

[3186] Do you play the flouting Jack?

1. 1. 170

[3187] Thrust thy neck into a yoke, wear the print of it and sigh away Sundays.

1. 1. 186-87

[3188] I neither feel how she should be loved, nor know how she should be worthy.

1. 1. 213-14

[3189] Thou wast ever an obstinate heretic in the despite of beauty.

1. 1. 217-18

[3190] The body of your discourse is sometime guarded with fragments, and the guards are but slightly basted on neither.

1. 1. 265-67

[3191] Ere you flout old ends any further, examine your conscience.

1. 1. 267-69

[3192] Thou wilt be like a lover presently,
And tire the hearer with a book of words.

1. 1. 286-87

[3193] Hath the fellow any wit that told you this?

1. 2. 15

[3194] I wonder that thou goest about to apply a moral medicine to a mortifying mischief.

1. 3. 10-12

I had rather be a canker in a hedge than a rose in his
grace.

[3195]

                               1. 3. 25 26

[He's been] trusted with a muzzle and enfranchised with
a clog.

[3196]

                              1. 3. 30-31

If I had my mouth I would bite.

[3197]

                              1. 3. 32-33

If I can cross him any way, I bless myself every way.

[3198]

                              1. 3. 63 64

How tartly that gentleman looks! I never can see him but
I am heart-burned an hour after.

[3199]

                              2. 1. 3-4

Lord, I could not endure a husband with a beard on his
face! I had rather lie in the woollen.

[3200]

                              2. 1. 26-28

What should I do with [a husband]? Dress him in my
apparel and make him my waiting-gentlewoman?

[3201]

                              2. 1. 30-31

He that is less than a man I am not for him.

[3202]

                              2. 1. 34-35

[I won't be fitted with a husband], not till God make men
of some other metal than earth. Would it not grieve a
woman to be over-mastered with a piece of valiant dust,
to make an account of her life to a clod of wayward marl?

[3203]

                              2. 1. 55-58

God keep him out of my sight when the dance is done!

[3204]

                              2. 1. 100-1

[3205] His gift is in devising impossible slanders.

2. 1. 128

[3206] None but libertines delight in him, and the commendation is not in his wit, but in his villainy.

2. 1. 128-30

[3207] He both pleases men and angers them, and then they laugh at him and beat him.

2. 1. 130-32

[3208] O, she misused me past the endurance of a block!

2. 1. 223

[3209] An oak with one green leaf on it would have answered her.

2. 1. 224-25

[3210] [You are] duller than a great thaw.

2. 1. 228

[3211] She speaks poniards, and every word stabs.

2. 1. 231-32

[3212] If her breath were as terrible as her terminations, there were no living near her, she would infect to the North Star.

2. 1. 232-34

[3213] I would not marry her, though she were endowed with all that Adam had left him before he transgressed.

2. 1. 234-36

[3214] She would have made Hercules have turned spit, yea, and have cleft his club to make the fire too.

2. 1. 236-38

While she is here, a man may live as quiet in hell as in a [3215] sanctuary, and people sin upon purpose, because they would go thither.

                                    2. 1. 241-43

I will fetch you a toothpicker now from the furthest inch [3216] of Asia; bring you the length of Prester John's foot; fetch you a hair off the great Cham's beard; do you any embassage to the Pygmies, rather than hold three words' conference with this harpy.

                                    2. 1. 250-54

Here's a dish I love not! I cannot endure my Lady [3217] Tongue.

                                    2. 1. 257-58

[This is the] mother of fools! [3218]

                                    2. 1. 268

[He is] civil as an orange, and something of that jealous [3219] complexion.

                                    2. 1. 276-77

If they were but a week married, they would talk them- [3220] selves mad.

                                    2. 1. 330-31

Whatsoever comes athwart his affection ranges evenly [3221] with mine.

                                    2. 2. 6-7

Only to despite them will I endeavour anything. [3222]

                                    2. 2. 31-32

[He will] become the argument of his own scorn. [3223]

                                    2. 3. 11

[3224] His words are a very fantastical banquet, just so many strange dishes.

2. 3. 20-21

[3225]   Tax not so bad a voice
To slander music any more than once.

2. 3. 44-45

[3226] If he had been a dog that should have howled thus, they would have hanged him.

2. 3. 79-80

[3227] That she loves him with an enraged affection, it is past the infinite of thought.

2. 3. 101-2

[3228] She will die ere she will bate one breath of her accustomed crossness.

2. 3. 170-73

[3229] The man, as you know all, hath a contemptible spirit.

2. 3. 175-76

[3230] He doth indeed show some sparks that are like wit.

2. 3. 180-81

[3231] In the managing of quarrels you may say he is wise; for either he avoids them with great discretion, or undertakes them with a most Christian-like fear.

2. 3. 183-86

[3232] I could wish he would modestly examine himelf.

2. 3. 200-1

[3233] [You are] merely a dumb-show.

2. 3. 210

I may chance have some odd quirks and remnants of wit [3234]
broken on me.

2. 3. 227-28

Shall quips and sentences and these paper bullets of the [3235]
brain awe a man from the career of his humour?

2. 3. 231-33

Against my will I am sent to bid you come in to dinner. [3236]

2. 3. 238-39

I took no more pains for those thanks than you take [3237]
pains to thank me.

2. 3. 241-42

She would spell him backward. [3238]

3. 1. 61

The gentleman should be her sister. [3239]

3. 1. 62

Nature, drawing of an antic, made a foul blot [in making [3240]
you].

3. 1. 63-64

[You are] a vane blown with all winds. [3241]

3. 1. 66

Such carping is not commendable. [3242]

3. 1. 71

To be so odd and from all fashions cannot be commend- [3243]
able.

3. 1. 72-73

There's no true drop of blood in him. [3244]

3. 2. 17-18

[3245] If he be sad, he wants money.

3. 2. 18-19

[3246] There is no appearance of fancy in him, unless it be a fancy that he hath to strange disguises.

3. 2. 29-30

[3247] The old ornament of his cheek hath already stuffed tennis-balls.

3. 2. 42-43

[3248] Disloyal? The word is too good to paint out her wickedness.

3. 2. 97-99

[3249] I could say she were worse; think you of a worse title and I will fit her to it.

3. 2. 99-100

[3250] You are thought here to be the most senseless and fit man for the [job].

3. 3. 22-23

[3251] Thank God you are rid of a knave.

3. 3. 30

[3252] You may suspect him to be no true man.

3. 3. 49-50

[3253] Like a true drunkard, utter all.

3. 3. 102-3

[3254] I may as well say the fool's a fool.

3. 3. 120

[3255] His codpiece seems as massy as his club.

3. 3. 134

We have here recovered the most dangerous piece of lechery that ever was known in the commonwealth.   [3256]

3. 3. 160-62

My cousin's a fool, and thou art another.   [3257]

3. 4. 10

I scorn that with my heels.   [3258]

3. 4. 46-47

[Your wit] is not seen enough, you should wear it in your cap.   [3259]

3. 4. 66-67

Thou prick'st her with a thistle.   [3260]

3. 4. 71

What pace is this that thy tongue keeps?   [3261]

3. 4. 87

His wits are not so blunt as, God help, I would desire they were.   [3262]

3. 5. 10-11

Comparisons are odorous.   [3263]

3. 5. 15

Neighbours, you are tedious.   [3264]

3. 5. 17

When the age is in, the wit is out.   [3265]

3. 5. 33

O, what men dare do! What men may do! What men daily do, not knowing what they do!   [3266]

4. 1. 18-19

[3267] Give not this rotten orange to your friend.

4. 1. 31

[3268] Her blush is guiltiness, not modesty.

4. 1. 41

[3269] You are more intemperate in your blood
Than Venus, or those pamper'd animals
That rage in savage sensuality.

4. 1. 59-61

[3270] Is my lord well that he doth speak so wide?

4. 1. 62

[3271] There is not chastity enough in language
Without offence to utter [her vile encounters].

4. 1. 97-98

[3272] I am sorry for thy much misgovernment.

4. 1. 99

[3273] Fair thee well, most foul.

4. 1. 103

[3274] This shame derives itself from unknown loins.

4. 1. 135

[3275] Why seek'st thou to cover with excuse
That which appears in proper nakedness?

4. 1. 174-75

[3276] Let all [his] sins lack mercy!

4. 1. 180

[3277] [He is] the bastard whose spirits toil in frame of villainies.

4. 1. 188-89

Will you not eat your word? [3278]

4. 1. 277

Is [he] not approved in the height a villain? [3279]

4. 1. 300

O God that I were a man! I would eat his heart in the [3280]
market-place.

4. 1. 305-6

Manhood is melted into curtsies, valour into compliment, [3281]
and men are only turned into tongue, and trim ones too.

4. 1. 318-20

He is now as valiant as Hercules that only tells a lie and [3282]
swears it.

4. 1. 320-21

I do not like thy look, I promise thee. [3283]

4. 2. 41-42

                    I pray thee cease thy counsel, [3284]
Which falls into mine ears as profitless
As water in a sieve.

5. 1. 3-5

[You] candle-wasters! [3285]

5. 1. 18

Men from children nothing differ. [3286]

5. 1. 33

There was never yet philosopher [3287]
That could endure a toothache patiently,
However they have writ the style of gods.

5. 1. 35-37

[3288] Tush, tush, man, never fleer and jest at me!

5. 1. 58

[3289] [You are] scambling, outfacing, fashion-monging boys,
That lie, and cog, and flout, deprave, and slander,
Go anticly, and show outward hideousness,
And speak off half a dozen dang'rous words,
How [you] might hurt [your] enemies, if [you] durst,
And this is all.

5. 1. 94-99

[3290] We had like to have had our noses snapped off with old
men without teeth.

5. 1. 115-16

[3291] He swore a thing to me on Monday night, which he for-
swore on Tuesday morning.

5. 1. 164-66

[3292] I will leave you now to your gossip-like humour.

5. 1. 182-83

[3293] You break jests as braggarts do their blades, which God
be thanked hurt not.

5. 1. 183-85

[3294] I must discontinue your company.

5. 1. 186-87

[3295] He goes in his doublet and hose and leaves off his wit!

5. 1. 196-97

[3296] What your wisdoms could not discover, these shallow
fools have brought to light.

5. 1. 227-29

        Let me see his eyes,   [3297]
That when I note another man like him
I may avoid him.

                                  5. 1. 253-55

Art thou the slave that with thy breath hast kill'd?   [3298]

                                  5. 1. 257

A most manly wit, it will not hurt a woman.   [3299]

                                  5. 2. 15-16

Foul words is but foul wind, and foul wind is but foul   [3300]
breath, and foul breath is noisome; therefore I will depart
unkissed.

                                  5. 2. 49-51

[Your bad parts] maintained so politic a state of evil that   [3301]
they will not admit any good part to intermingle with
them.

                                  5. 2. 58-6

        You have such a February face,   [3302]
So full of frost, of storm, and cloudiness.

                                  5. 4. 41-42

Some such strange bull leap'd your father's cow,   [3303]
And got a calf in that same noble feat
Much like to you, for you have just his bleat.

                                  5. 4. 49-51

A college of wit-crackers cannot flout me out of my hu- [3304]
mour.

                                  5. 4. 99-100

If a man will be beaten with brains, [he] shall wear noth- [3305]
ing handsome about him.

                                  5. 4. 101-3

Othello

[3306] Mere prattle without practice.

1. 1. 26

[3307] If thou wilt needs damn thyself, do it a more delicate way
than drowning; make all the money thou canst.

1. 3. 354-55

[3308] I mine own gain'd knowledge should profane,
If I would time expend with such a snipe,
But for my sport and profit.

1. 3. 382-84

[3309] [He] will as tenderly be led by the nose as asses are.

1. 3. 399-400

[3310] Sir, would she give you so much of her lips as of her
tongue she oft bestows on me, you'd have enough.

2. 1. 100-2

[3311] She puts her tongue a little in her heart, and chides with
thinking.

2. 1. 106-7

You are pictures out o' doors;   [3312]
Bells in your parlours; wild-cats in your kitchens;
Saints in your injuries; devils being offended;
Players in your housewifery; and housewives in your
        beds.

                                              2. 1. 109-12

You rise to play, and go to bed to work.   [3313]

                                              2. 1. 115

It had been better you had not kiss'd your three fingers   [3314]
so oft, which now again you are most apt to play the sir
in.

                                              2. 1. 172-74

[He is] a subtle slippery knave, a finder out of occasions;   [3315]
that has an eye can stamp and counterfeit the true
advantages never present themselves!

                                              2. 1. 240-42

[You are] an index and prologue to the history of lust and   [3316]
foul thoughts.

                                              2. 1. 254-55

[Thou art] as full of quarrel and offence as my young   [3317]
mistress' dog.

                                              2. 3. 46-47

[Thou] hath to-night carous'd potations pottle-deep.   [3318]

                                              2. 3. 49-50

[You] are most potent in potting.   [3319]

                                              2. 3. 71-72

Dost thou prate, rogue?   [3320]

                                              2. 3. 143

[3321]
              What's the matter,
That you unlace your reputation thus,
And spend your rich opinion, for the name
Of a night-brawler?

2. 3. 184-87

[3322] [He] so likes your music, that he desires you, of all loves,
to make no more noise with it.

3. 1. 11

[3323] If you have any music that may not be heard, to 't again.

3. 1. 16

[3324] Dost thou hear, mine honest friend?
No, I hear not your honest friend, I hear you.

3. 1. 21-22

[3325]
              O curse of marriage,
That we can call these delicate creatures ours,
And not their appetites! I had rather be a toad,
And live upon the vapour in a dungeon,
Than keep a corner in a thing I love,
For others' uses.

3. 3. 272-77

[3326] Thou hadst been better have been born a dog,
Than answer my wak'd wrath.

3. 3. 368-69

[3327] O that the slave had forty thousand lives!
One is too poor, too weak for my revenge.

3. 3. 449-50

[3328] Damn her, lewd minx!

3. 3. 482

Here's a young and sweating devil here,   [3329]
That commonly rebels.

                                        3. 4. 38-39

'Tis not a year or two shows us a man: [3330]
They are all but stomachs, and we all but food;
They eat us hungerly, and when they are full,
They belch us.

                                        3. 4. 100-3

            Go to, woman,   [3331]
Throw your vile guesses in the devil's teeth
From whence you have them; you are jealous now.

                                    3. 4. 181-83

You are all in all in spleen,   [3332]
And nothing of a man.

                                        4. 1. 88-89

If that the earth could teem with women's tears,   [3333]
Each drop she falls would prove a crocodile.

                                    4. 1. 240-41

Goats and monkeys!   [3334]
                                        4. 1. 259

Are his wits safe? Is he not light of brain?   [3335]
                                        4. 1. 265

There's no man happy, the purest of her sex   [3336]
Is foul as slander.

                                    4. 2. 18-19

            This is a subtle whore,   [3337]
A closet, lock and key, of villainous secrets.

                                    4. 2. 21-22

[3338] Heaven truly knows, that thou art false as hell.

4. 2. 40

[3339] O, thou black weed, why art so lovely fair?
Thou smell'st so sweet, that the sense aches at thee,
Would thou hadst ne'er been born!

4. 2. 69-71

[3340] A halter pardon him, and hell gnaw his bones!

4. 2. 138

[3341] Put in every honest hand a whip,
To lash the rascal naked through the world!

4. 2. 144-45

[3342]   O, these men, these men!
Dost thou in conscience think
That there be women do abuse their husbands
In such gross kind?

4. 3. 59-62

[3343] I have rubb'd this young quat almost to the sense,
And he grows angry.

5. 1. 11-12

[3344] She's like a liar gone to burning hell.

5. 2. 130

[3345] She was false as water.

5. 2. 135

[3346] May his pernicious soul rot half a grain a day!

5. 2. 156-57

[3347] O gull, o dolt, as ignorant as dirt!

5. 2. 164-65

What should such a fool do with so good a woman?   [3348]

5. 2. 234-35

Every puny whipster gets my sword.   [3349]

5. 2. 245

Pericles

[3350] All the whole heap must die.

1. 1. 34

[3351] Here they stand martyrs slain in Cupid's wars.

1. 1. 39

[3352] I will gloze with him.

1. 1. 111

[3353] How courtesy would seem to cover sin!

1. 1. 122

[3354] Both like serpents are, who though they feed
On sweetest flowers, yet they poison breed.

1. 1. 133-34

[3355] 'Tis time to fear when tyrants seem to kiss.

1. 2. 79

[3356] Thou speak'st like him's untutor'd to repeat:
Who makes the fairest show means most deceit.

1. 4. 74-75

What, ho, Pilch! What, Patch-breech, I say!   [3357]

> 2. 1. 12-14

A plague on them, they ne'er come but I look to be   [3358]
wash'd!

> 2. 1. 25-26

I can compare our rich misers to nothing so fitly as to a   [3359]
whale: he plays and tumbles, driving the poor fry before
him, and at last devours them all at a mouthful.

> 2. 1. 29-31

We would purge the land of these drones, that rob the   [3360]
bee of her honey.

> 2. 1. 46-47

What a drunken knave was the sea to cast thee in our   [3361]
way!

> 2. 1. 57-58

O, sir, things must be as they may; and what a man   [3362]
cannot get, he may lawfully deal for his wife's soul.

> 2. 1. 112-14

> They are like to gnats   [3363]
Which make a sound, but kill'd are wonder'd at.

> 2. 3. 62-63

[You are] relish'd of a base descent.   [3364]

> 2. 5. 59

Thou art the rudeliest welcome to this world.   [3365]

> 3. 1. 30

[You] poor inch of nature!   [3366]

> 3. 1. 34

[3367] 'Tis a good constraint of fortune
It belches upon us.

3. 2. 55-56

[3368] They with continual action are even as good as rotten.

4. 2. 8-9

[3369] The stuff we have, a strong wind will blow it to pieces,
they are so pitifully sodden.

4. 2. 17-18

[3370] She quickly poop'd him; she made him roastmeat for
worms.

4. 2. 22-23

[3371] Such a maidenhead were no cheap thing, if men were as
they have been.

4. 2. 56-57

[3372] Thunder shall not so awake the bed of eels as my giving
out her beauty stirs up the lewdly inclin'd.

4. 2. 140-42

[3373]   He did not flow
From honourable sources.

4. 3. 27-28

[3374] [Your face] was blurted at and held a malkin [slut]
Not worth the time of day.

4. 3. 34-35

[3375]   Thou art like the harpy,
Which, to betray, dost with thine angel's face,
Seize with thine eagle's talons.

4. 3. 46-48

No visor does become black villainy [3376]
So well as soft and tender flattery.

4. 4. 44-45

She's able to freeze the god Priapus, and undo a whole [3377]
generation.

4. 6. 3-4

She would make a puritan of the devil, if he would [3378]
cheapen a kiss of her.

4. 6. 9-10

Faith, I must ravish her, or she'll disfurnish us of all our [3379]
cavalleria, and make our swearers priests.

4. 6. 11-12

The pox upon her green-sickness for me! [3380]

4. 6. 13

[You] peevish baggage! [3381]

4. 6. 17-18

She would serve after a long voyage at sea. [3382]

4. 6. 42

The house you dwell in proclaims you to be a creature of [3383]
sale.

4. 6. 76-77

Most ungentle fortune [3384]
Have plac'd me in this sty, where, since I came,
Diseases have been sold dearer than physic.

4. 6. 95-97

[Your] very doors and windows savour vilely. [3385]

4. 6. 110

[3386] Avaunt thou damned door-keeper! Your house,
But for this virgin that doth prop it,
Would sink and overwhelm you.

4. 6. 118-20

[3387] Your peevish chastity is not worth a breakfast in the
cheapest country under the cope.

4. 6. 122-24

[3388] She makes our profession as it were to stink afore the
face of the gods.

4. 6. 135-36

[3389] Thou hold'st a place, for which the pained'st fiend
Of hell would not in reputation change.

4. 6. 162-63

[3390] Thou art the damned door-keeper to every
Coistrel that comes inquiring for his Tib;
To the choleric fisting of every rogue
Thy ear is liable.

4. 6. 164-67

[3391]   Thy food is such
As hath been belch'd on by infected lungs.

4. 6. 167-68

[3392] Do any thing but this thou doest. Empty
Old receptacles, or common shores, of filth;
Serve by indenture to the common hangman:
Any of these ways are yet better than this;
For what thou professest, a baboon, could he speak,
Would own a name too dear.

4. 6. 173-78

Richard II

With a foul traitor's name stuff I thy throat. [3393]

                                        1. 1. 44

I do defy him, and I spit at him, [3394]
Call him a slanderous coward, and a villain.

                                        1. 1. 60-61

God and good men hate so foul a liar. [3395]

                                        1. 1. 114

As low as to thy heart through the false passage of thy [3396]
throat thou liest.

                                        1. 1. 124-25

It issues from the rancour of a villain, [3397]
A recreant and most degenerate traitor.

                                        1. 1. 143-44

[You] are but gilded loam, or painted clay. [3398]

                                        1. 1. 179

Since thou hast far to go, bear not along the clogging [3399] burden of a guilty soul.

1. 3. 198-99

[3400] Now put it, God, in the physician's mind
To help him to his grave immediately!

1. 4. 59-60

[3401] All in vain comes counsel to his ear.

2. 1. 4

[3402] [You] rough rug-headed kerns, which live like venom!

2. 1. 156-57

[3403] [He] is not himself, but basely led by flatterers.

2. 1. 241-42

[3404] That word "grace" in an ungracious mouth is but profane.

2. 3. 87-88

[3405] [You] caterpillars of the commonwealth!

2. 3. 165

[3406] His treasons will sit blushing in his face.

3. 2. 51

[3407] Boys, with women's voices, strive to speak big.

3. 2. 113-14

[3408] [You are] dogs easily won to fawn on any man!

3. 2. 130

[3409] [You are] snakes, in my heart-blood warm'd, that sting
my heart!

3. 2. 131

[3410] Judases, each one thrice worse than Judas!

3. 2. 132

Terrible hell, make war upon their spotted souls for this!   [3411]
>3. 2. 134-35

[They are] noisome weeds which without profit suck   [3412]
The soil's fertility from wholesome flowers.
>3. 4. 38-39

How dares thy harsh rude tongue sound this unpleasing   [3413]
news?
>3. 4. 74

Thou little better thing than earth!   [3414]
>3. 4. 78

I know your daring tongue scorns to unsay what once it   [3415]
hath delivered.
>4. 1. 8-9

What answer shall I make to this base man?   [3416]
Shall I so much dishonour my fair stars
On equal terms to give him chastisement?
>4. 1. 20-22

May [your] hands rot off!   [3417]
>4. 1. 49

I have a thousand spirits in one breast   [3418]
To answer twenty thousand such as you.
>4. 1. 58-59

Spit upon him whilst I say he lies, and lies, and lies.   [3419]
>4. 1. 75-76

       O forfend it, God,   [3420]
That in a Christian climate souls refin'd
Should show so heinous, black, obscene a deed!
>4. 1. 129-31

[3421] If thy offences were upon record,
Would it not shame thee, in so fair a troop,
To read a lecture of them?

4. 1. 230-32

[3422] You Pilates have here deliver'd me to my sour cross,
And water cannot wash away your sin.

4. 1. 240-42

[3423] Thou haught insulting man!

4. 1. 254

[3424] Fiend, thou torments me ere I come to hell.

4. 1. 270

[3425] He daily doth frequent with unrestrained loose companions.

5. 3. 6-7

[3426] They do plot unlikely wonders.

5. 5. 18-19

[3427] Bear a burden like an ass!

5. 5. 93

[3428] Go thou and fill another room in hell.

5. 5. 107

Richard III

[You're] not shap'd for sportive tricks,　　　　[3429]
Nor made to court an amorous looking-glass.

　　　　　　　　　　1. 1. 14-15

[What] mighty gossips!　　　　[3430]

　　　　　　　　1. 1. 83

More direful hap betide that hated wretch　　　　[3431]
Than I can wish to adders, spiders, toads,
Or any creeping venomed thing that lives.

　　　　　　　　　1. 2. 17-20

Foul devil, for God's sake hence, and trouble us not;　　　　[3432]
For thou hast made the happy earth thy hell,
Fill'd it with cursing cries and deep exclaims.

　　　　　　　　　1. 2. 50-52

Thou lump of foul deformity!　　　　[3433]

　　　　　　　　1. 2. 57

O wonderful, when devils tell the truth!　　　　[3434]

　　　　　　　　1. 2. 73

[3435] [You] diffus'd infection of a man!

1. 2. 78

[3436] Fouler than heart can think thee, thou canst make
No excuse current but to hang thyself.

1. 2. 83-84

[3437] Thou art unfit for any place but hell.

1. 2. 111

[3438] Never hung poison on a fouler toad.

1. 2. 151

[3439] Out of my sight! Thou dost infect my eyes.

1. 2. 152

[3440] God grant we never may have need of you.

1. 3. 76

[3441]   I have too long borne
Your blunt upbraidings and your bitter scoffs.

1. 3. 103-4

[3442] Hie thee to hell for shame, and leave this world,
Thou cacodemon: there thy kingdom is.

1. 3. 143-4

[3443] This sorrow that I have by right is yours.

1. 3. 172

[3444] If heaven have any grievous plague in store
Exceeding those that I can wish upon thee,
O, let them keep it till thy sins be ripe,
And then hurl down their indignation
On thee, the troubler of the poor world's peace.

1. 3. 217-21

The worm of conscience still begnaw thy soul.   [3445]

1. 3. 222

No sleep close up that deadly eye of thine,   [3446]
Unless it be while some tormenting dream
Affrights thee with a hell of ugly devils.

1. 3. 225-27

Thou elvish-mark'd, abortive, rooting hog,   [3447]
Thou that wast seal'd in thy nativity
The slave of Nature, and the son of hell;
Thou slander of thy heavy mother's womb,
Thou loathed issue of thy father's loins,
Thou rag of honour!

1. 3. 228-33

Poor painted queen, vain flourish of my fortune: [3448]
Why strew'st thou sugar on that bottled spider,
Whose deadly web ensnareth thee about?
Fool, fool; thou whet'st a knife to kill thyself.

1. 3. 241-44

[You] poisonous hunch-back'd toad!   [3449]

1. 3. 246

Dispute not with her; she is a lunatic.   [3450]

1. 3. 254

You are malapert.   [3451]

1. 3. 255

Sin, death, and hell have set their marks on him,   [3452]
And all their ministers attend on him.

1. 3. 293-94

[You] simple gulls!   [3453]

1. 3. 328

[3454] Thus [you] clothe [your] naked villainy
With odd old ends stol'n forth of Holy Writ,
And seem a saint, when most [you] play the devil.

1. 3. 336-38

[3455] Thy voice is thunder, but thy looks are humble.

1. 4. 158

[3456] [You are] deep, hollow, treacherous, and full of guile.

2. 1. 38

[3457] [You] incapable and shallow innocents!

2. 2. 18

[3458] Ah, that Deceit should steal such gentle shape
And with a virtuous vizor hide deep Vice!

2. 2. 27-28

[3459] Fie, what a slug is [he].

3. 1. 22

[3460] Here comes the sweating lord.

3. 1. 24

[3461] You are too senseless-obstinate,
Too ceremonious and traditional.
Weigh it but with the grossness of this age.

3. 1. 44-46

[3462] A knot you are of damned bloodsuckers.

3. 3. 6

[3463] [You are] dangerous and unsuspected.

3. 5. 23

[3464] Who is so gross that cannot see this palpable device?

3. 6. 10-11

What tongueless blocks were they! [3465]

3. 7. 42

Thy mother's name is ominous to children. [3466]

4. 1. 39

Thou wast not wont to be so dull. [3467]

4. 2. 17

[Your] humble means match not [your] haughty spirit. [3468]

4. 2. 37

Gold were as good as twenty orators,
And will, no doubt, tempt him to anything. [3469]

4. 2. 38-39

Drop into the rotten mouth of death. [3470]

4. 4. 2

From forth the kennel of thy womb hath crept [3471]
A hell-hound that doth hunt us all to death.

4. 4. 47-48

[You are a] foul defacer of God's handiwork. [3472]

4. 4. 53

Earth gapes, hell burns, fiends roar, saints pray, [3473]
To have him suddenly convey'd from hence.
Cancel his bond of life, dear God I pray,
That I may live and say, 'the dog is dead.'

4. 4. 75-78

That bottled spider, that foul bunch-back'd toad! [3474]

4. 4. 81

Thou cam'st on earth to make the earth my hell. [3475]

4. 4. 167

[3476] Take with thee my most grievous curse.

4. 4. 188

[3477] No doubt the murd'rous knife was dull and blunt
Till it was whetted on thy stone-hard heart.

4. 4. 227-28

[3478] That my nails were anchor'd in thine eyes!

4. 4. 232

[3479] The world—'Tis full of thy foul wrongs.

4. 4. 374

[3480] [You] wretched, bloody, and usurping boar!

5. 2. 7

[3481] My conscience hath a thousand several tongues,
And every tongue brings in a several tale,
And every tale condemns [you] for a villain.

5. 3. 194-96

[3482] [Here's] a sort of vagabonds, rascals, and runaways;
A scum of Bretons and base lackey peasants,
Whom their o'er-cloyed country vomits forth.

5. 3. 317-19

[3483] A milksop! One that never in his life
Felt so much cold as over-shoes in snow.

5. 3. 326-27

[3484] These overwheening rags of France!

5. 3. 329

Romeo and Juliet

Draw your neck out of your collar.   [3485]

                           1. 1. 4

Draw thy tool. My naked weapon is out.   [3486]

                     1. 1. 30-32

[I] breathe defiance to [your] ears.   [3487]

                       1. 1. 108

Hiss him in scorn.   [3488]

                       1. 1. 110

Beauty starv'd with [your] severity   [3489]
Cuts beauty off from all posterity.

                    1. 1. 217-18

O teach me how I should forget to think.   [3490]

                       1. 1. 224

Thou wilt fall backward when thou hast more wit.   [3491]

                    1. 3. 42

[3492] He's a man of wax.

1. 3. 76

[3493]   What care I
What curious eye doth quote deformities?

1. 4. 30-31

[3494] Candle-holder!

1. 4. 38

[3495] Tut, dun's the mouse.

1. 4. 40

[3496] [You] small grey-coated gnat.

1. 4. 67

[3497] [He's] not half so big as a round little worm.

1. 4. 68

[3498] [He] bakes the elf-locks in foul sluttish hairs.

1. 4. 90

[3499] [They are] the children of an idle brain,
Begot of nothing but vain fantasy,
Which is as thin of substance as the air
And more inconstant than the wind.

1. 4. 97-100

[3500] When good manners shall lie all in one or two men's
hands, and they unwashed too, 'tis a foul thing.

1. 5. 3-5

[3501]   What, dares the slave
Come hither, cover'd with an antic face,
To fleer and scorn at our solemnity?

1. 5. 54-56

You kiss by th' book.   [3502]

1. 5. 109

He heareth not, he stirreth not, he moveth not: [3503]
The ape is dead.

2. 1. 15-16

Blind is his love, and best befits the dark.   [3504]

2. 1. 32

O that she were   [3505]
An open-arse and thou a poperin pear!

2. 1. 37-38

Her vestal livery is but sick and green   [3506]
And none but fools do wear it.

2. 2. 8-9

She speaks, yet she says nothing.   [3507]

2. 2. 12

Young men's love then lies   [3508]
Not truly in their hearts but in their eyes.

2. 3. 63-64

He is already dead, stabbed with a white wench's black   [3509]
eye, run through the ear with a love song, the very pin of
his heart cleft with the blind bow-boy's butt-shaft.

2. 4. 13-16

O, he's the courageous captain of compliments.   [3510]

2. 4. 19-20

[You're] the very butcher of a silk button!   [3511]

2. 4. 23

The pox of such antic lisping affecting phantasimes,   [3512] these new tuners of accent!

2. 4. 28-29

[3513] These strange flies, these fashion-mongers, these 'pardon-me's'!

2. 4. 32-33

[3514] O flesh, flesh, how art thou fishified.

2. 4. 38-39

[3515] In such a case as mine a man may strain courtesy.

2. 4. 52-53

[3516] O single-soled jest, solely singular for the singleness.

2. 4. 67-68

[3517] If our wits run the wild-goose chase I am done. For thou hast more of the wild-goose in one of thy wits than I am sure I have in my whole five.

2. 4. 72-74

[3518] I will bite thee by the ear for that jest.

2. 4. 78

[3519] Thy wit is a very bitter sweeting, it is a most sharp sauce.

2. 4. 80-81

[3520] This drivelling love is like a great natural that runs lolling up and down to hide his bauble in a hole.

2. 4. 91-93

[3521] [A fan] to hide her face, for her fan's the fairer face!

2. 4. 106-7

[3522] [Your wit] is something stale and hoar ere it be spent.

2. 4. 130-31

What saucy merchant was this, that was so full of his
ropery?

[3523]

              2. 4. 142-43

[He's] a gentleman that loves to hear himself talk, and
will speak more in a minute than he will stand to in a
month.

[3524]

              2. 4. 144-46

Scurvy knave! I am none of his flirt-gills [loose women], I
am none of his skains-mates [cut-throat companions].

[3525]

              2. 4. 150-51

If ye should lead her in a fool's paradise, as they say, it
were a very gross kind of behaviour, as they say.

[3526]

              2. 4. 162-64

She, good soul, had as lief see a toad, a very toad, as see
him.

[3527]

              2. 4. 198-99

Thou sham'st the music of sweet news
By playing it to me with so sour a face.

[3528]

              2. 5. 23-24

He is not the flower of courtesy.

[3529]

              2. 5. 43

Thou art as hot a Jack in thy mood as any in Italy.

[3530]

              3. 1. 11

Why, thou wilt quarrel with a man that hath a hair more
or a hair less in his beard than thou hast. Thou wilt
quarrel with a man for cracking nuts, having no other
reason but because thou hast hazel eyes. What eye but
such an eye would spy out such a quarrel?

[3531]

              3. 1. 16-21

[3532] Thy head is as full of quarrels as an egg is full of meat.

3. 1. 22

[3533] What, dost thou make us minstrels? If thou make minstrels of us, look to hear nothing but discords.

3. 1. 45-47

[3534] The love I bear thee can afford no better term than this: thou art a villain.

3. 1. 59-60

[3535] Villain am I none, therefore farewell. I see thou knowest me not.

3. 1. 63-64

[3536] O calm, dishonourable, vile submission.

3. 1. 72

[3537] You rat-catcher!

3. 1. 74

[3538] Good King of Cats, [I wouldst have] nothing but one of your nine lives [and] dry-beat the rest of the eight.

3. 1. 76-78

[3539] [You are] a braggart, a rogue, a villain, that fights by the book of arithmetic.

3. 1. 102-4

[3540] They have made worms' meat of me.

3. 1. 109

[3541] Away to heaven respective lenity
And fire-ey'd fury be my conduct now!

3. 1. 125-26

Where are the vile beginners of this fray? [3542]

3. 1. 143

Thou sober-suited matron. [3543]

3. 2. 11

What devil art thou that dost torment me thus? [3544]
This torture should be roar'd in dismal hell.

3. 2. 43-44

O serpent heart, hid with a flowering face. [3545]
Did ever dragon keep so fair a cave?

3. 2. 73-74

Beautiful tyrant, fiend angelical, [3546]
Dove-feather'd raven, wolvish-ravening lamb!

3. 2. 75-76

Blister'd be thy tongue for such a wish. [3547]

3. 2. 90-91

Thou cut'st my head off with a golden axe [3548]
And smilest upon the stroke that murders me.

3. 3. 22-23

More validity, more honourable state, more courtship [3549]
lives in carrion flies.

3. 3. 33-35

Unseemly woman in a seeming man, [3550]
And ill-beseeming beast in seeming both!

3. 3. 111-12

Thy noble shape is but a form of wax [3551]
Digressing from the valour of a man.

3. 3. 125-26

[3552] Hang thee young baggage!

3. 5. 160

[3553] Smatter with your gossips, go.

3. 5. 171

[3554] Peace, you mumbling fool!
Utter your gravity o'er the gossip's bowl,
For here we need it not.

3. 5. 173-75

[3555] A wretched puling fool, a whining mammet!

3. 5. 183-84

[3556] Graze where you will, you shall not house with me.

3. 5. 188

[3557] Hang! Beg! Starve! Die in the streets!

3. 5. 192

[3558] [What's] this borrow'd likeness of shrunk death!

4. 1. 104

[3559] A peevish self-will'd harlotry it is.

4. 2. 14

[3560] How now, my headstrong: where have you been gadding?

4. 2. 16

[3561] [Your] foul mouth no healthsome air breathes in.

4. 3. 34

[3562] [I'll give you] no money, on my faith, but the gleek!

4. 5. 112

[3563] Pray you put up your dagger and put out your wit.

4. 5. 119

I will dry-beat you with an iron wit.   [3564]
Answer me like men.

4. 5. 120-21

What a pestilent knave is this same.   [3565]

4. 5. 139

Thou detestable maw, thou womb of death.   [3566]

5. 3. 45

Thus I enforce thy rotten jaws to open,   [3567]
And in despite I'll cram thee with more food.

5. 3. 47-48

Remain with worms that are thy chambermaids.   [3568]

5. 3. 108-9

The Taming of the Shrew

[3569] Y'are a baggage.

Ind. 1. 3

[3570] O monstrous beast, how like a swine he lies!

Ind. 1. 32

[3571] How foul and loathsome is thine image!

Ind. 1. 33

[3572] [He is] by birth a pedlar, by education a cardmaker, by transmutation a bear-herd, and now by present profession a tinker.

Ind. 2. 18-21

[3573]   [My] care should be
To comb your noddle with a three-legg'd stool.

1. 1. 63-64

[3574] Thinkest thou, though her father be very rich, any man is so very a fool to be married to hell?

1. 1. 123-25

There's small choice in rotten apples.   [3575]

1. 1. 134-35

Woo her, wed her, and bed her, and rid the house of her.   [3576]

1. 1. 144-45

I'll knock your knave's pate.   [3577]

1. 2. 12

Why, give him gold enough and marry him to a puppet or   [3578]
an aglet-baby, or an old trot with ne'er a tooth in her
head, though she have as many diseases as two and fifty
horses.

1. 2. 77-80

Her only fault, and that is faults enough,   [3579]
Is that she is intolerable curst,
And shrewd, and froward, so beyond all measure.

1. 2. 87-89

I know she is an irksome brawling scold.   [3580]

1. 2. 186

Will you woo this wildcat?   [3581]

1. 2. 195

And do you tell me of a woman's tongue,   [3582]
That gives not half so great a blow to hear
As will a chestnut in a farmer's fire?

1. 2. 206-8

Tush, tush, fear boys with bugs!   [3583]

1. 2. 209

Lead apes in hell!   [3584]

2. 1. 34

[3585] She did call me rascal fiddler
And twangling Jack with twenty such vile terms,
As had she studied to misuse me so.

2. 1. 157-59

[3586] Let him that mov'd you hither
Remove you hence. I knew you at the first
You were a movable.

2. 1. 195-97

[3587] Asses are made to bear, and so are you.

2. 1. 199

[3588] Well ta'en, and like a buzzard.

2. 1. 206

[3589] If I be waspish, best beware my sting.

2. 1. 210

[3590] What is your crest, a coxcomb?

2. 1. 223

[3591] [You are] rough, and coy, and sullen.

2. 1. 237

[3592] Go, fool, and whom thou keep'st command.

2. 1. 251

[3593] [You are] one half lunatic,
A madcap ruffian and a swearing Jack,
That thinks with oaths to face the matter out.

2. 1. 280-82

[3594] If she be curst it is for policy.

2. 1. 285

Greybeard, thy love doth freeze. [3595]

2. 1. 331

A vengeance on your crafty wither'd hide! [3596]

2. 1. 397

'Tis the base knave that jars. [3597]

3. 1. 45

[You are] a mad-brain rudesby, full of spleen. [3598]

3. 2. 10

       He was a frantic fool,
Hiding his bitter jests in blunt behaviour. [3599]

3. 2. 12-13

Such an injury would vex a saint,
Much more a shrew of thy impatient humour. [3600]

3. 2. 28-29

[He is] possessed with the glanders and like to mose in [3601]
the chine, troubled with the lampass, infected with the
fashions, full of windgalls, sped with spavins, rayed with
the yellows, past cure of the fives, stark spoiled with the
staggers, begnawn with the bots, swayed in the back and
shoulder-shotten, near-legged before, and with a half-
cheeked bit and a headstall of sheep's leather, which,
being restrained to keep him from stumbling, hath been
often burst and new-repaired with knots; one girth six
times pieced and a woman's crupper of velure, which
hath two letters for her name fairly set down in studs,
and here and there pieced with pack-thread.

3. 2. 48-61

[You are] a monster, a very monster in apparel. [3602]

3. 2. 67-69

[36030] You three-inch fool!

4. 1. 23

[3604] Am I but three inches? Why, thy horn is a foot, and so long am I at the least.

4. 1. 24-25

[3605] You logger-headed and unpolish'd grooms!

4. 1. 112

[3606] What, no attendance? No regard? No duty?

4. 1. 113

[3607] You peasant swain! You whoreson malt-horse drudge!

4. 1. 116

[3608] [You] whoreson beetle-headed, flap-ear'd knave!

4. 1. 144

[3609] You heedless joltheads and unmanner'd slaves!

4. 1. 153

[3610] Sorrow on thee and all the pack of you
That triumph thus upon my misery!

4. 3. 33-34

[3611] Fie, fie! 'Tis lewd and filthy.

4. 3. 65

[3612] O monstrous arrogance! Thou liest, thou thread, thou
        thimble,
Thou yard, three-quarters, half-yard, quarter, nail,
Thou flea, thou nit, thou winter-cricket thou!

4. 3. 107-10

[3613] Brav'd in mine own house with a skein of thread?
Away, thou rag, thou quantity, thou remnant,

Or I shall so bemete thee with thy yard
As thou shalt think on prating whilst thou liv'st!

4. 3. 111-14

O, I am undone, I am undone! While I play the good [3614]
husband at home, my son and my servant spend all at
the university!

5. 1. 59-62

Thus strangers may be haled and abused. [3615]

5. 1. 98

I'll slit the villain's nose! [3616]

5. 1. 120

Am I your bird? I mean to shift my bush. [3617]

5. 2. 46

[He has] a good swift simile, but something currish. [3618]

5. 2. 54

A woman mov'd is like a fountain troubled, [3619]
Muddy, ill-seeming, thick, bereft of beauty.

5. 2. 143-44

[You are] froward, peevish, sullen, sour! [3620]

5. 2. 158

The Tempest

[3621]   His complexion is perfect gallows.

1. 1. 29

[3622]   A pox o' your throat, you bawling, blasphemous,
inchartable dog!

1. 1. 40-41

[3623]   Hang, cur! hang, you whoreson, insolent noise-maker!

1. 1. 43-44

[3624]   [You are] as leaky as an unstanched wench.

1. 1. 47-48

[3625]   [He] made such a sinner of his memory,
To credit his own lie.

1. 2. 101-2

[3626]   Hell is empty,
And all the devils are here.

1. 2. 214-15

[3627]   Thou liest, malignant thing!

1. 2. 257

[You] freckled whelp hag-born! [3628]

1. 2. 283

[You] slave, who never yields us kind answer! [3629]

1. 2. 310-11

'Tis a villain, sir, I do not love to look on. [3630]

1. 2. 311-12

Toads, beetles, bats, light on you! [3631]

1. 2. 342

Thou most lying slave, [3632]
Whom stripes may move, not kindness! I have us'd thee,
Filth as thou art, with human care.

1. 2. 346-48

Abhorred slave, [3633]
Which any print of goodness wilt not take,
Being capable of all ill!

1. 2. 353-55

Thou didst not, savage, [3634]
Know thine own meaning, but wouldst gabble like
A thing most brutish.

1. 2. 357-59

You taught me language; and my profit on 't [3635]
Is, I know how to curse. The red plague rid you
For learning me your language!

1. 2. 365-67

[3636]

Hag-seed, hence!

1. 2. 367

What! I say, my foot a tutor? [3637]

1. 2. 471-72

[3638] Silence! one word more
Shall make me chide thee, if not hate thee.

1. 2. 478-79

[3639] He receives comfort like cold porridge.

2. 1. 10

[3640] Look, he's winding up the watch of his wit; by and by it will strike.

2. 1. 12-13

[3641] Fie, what a spendthrift is he of his tongue!

2. 1. 23

[3642] The air breathes upon us here most sweetly.
As if it had lungs, and rotten ones.
Or as 'twere perfum'd by a fen.

2. 1. 45-47

[3643] He misses not much.
No; he doth but mistake the truth totally.

2. 1. 54-55

[3644] What impossible matter will he make easy next?

2. 1. 85

[3645] You cram these words into mine ears against the stomach of my sense.

2. 1. 102-3

[3646] What strange fish hath made his meal on thee?

2. 1. 108-9

[3647] Thou dost talk nothing to me.

2. 1. 166

[3648] These gentlemen are of such sensible and nimble lungs that they always use to laugh at nothing.

2, 1. 168-70

I will not adventure my discretion so weakly.   [3649]

2. 1. 182-83

       Thou dost snore distinctly;   [3650]
There's meaning in thy snores.

2. 1. 212-13

Hereditary sloth instructs [you].   [3651]

2. 1. 218

All the infections that the sun sucks up   [3652]
From bogs, fens, flats, on [him] fall, and make him
By inch-meal a disease!

2. 2. 1-3

What have we here? a man or a fish? dead or alive?   [3653]

2. 2. 24-25

He smells like a fish; a very ancient and fish-like smell; a   [3654]
kind of, not of the newest Poor-John.

2. 2. 25-28

Any strange beast there makes a man.   [3655]

2. 2. 32

When they will not give a doit to relieve a lame beggar,   [3656]
they will lay out ten to see a dead Indian.

2. 2. 32-34

This is a very scurvy tune to sing at a man's funeral.   [3657]

2. 2. 45

He's in his fit now, and does not talk after the wisest.   [3658]

2. 2. 75-76

[3659] His forward voice, now, is to speak well of his friend; his backward voice is to utter foul speeches and to detract.

2. 2. 91-94

[3660] Doth thy other mouth call me?

2. 2. 98

[3661] Though thou canst swim like a duck, thou art made like a goose.

2. 2. 131-32

[3662] By this good light, this is a very shallow monster!

2. 2. 144

[3663] I shall laugh myself to death at this puppy-headed monster. A most scurvy monster! I could find in my heart to beat him.

2. 2. 154-56

[3664] He's compos'd of harshness.

3. 1. 9

[3665] Such baseness had never like executor.

3. 1. 12-13

[3666] Sit lazy by.

3. 1. 28

[3667] Poor worm, thou art infected!

3. 1. 31

[3668] [You] prattle something too wildly.

3. 1. 57-58

[3669] [You] patient log-man.

3. 1. 67

If [the others] be brain'd like [you], the state totters.   [3670]

3. 2. 6

My man-monster hath drown'd his tongue in sack.   [3671]

3. 2. 11

You'll lie, like dogs, and yet say nothing neither.   [3672]

3. 2. 18-19

I'll not serve him, he is not valiant.   [3673]

3. 2. 22-23

Thou debosh'd fish, thou!   [3674]

3. 2. 25

Bite him to death, I prithee.   [3675]

3. 2. 32

By this hand, I will supplant some of your teeth.   [3676]

3. 2. 47-48

I do beseech thy greatness, give him blows,   [3077]
And take his bottle from him: when that's gone,
He shall drink nought but brine.

3. 2. 63-65

By this hand, I'll turn my mercy out o' doors, and make a   [3678]
stock-fish of thee.

3. 2. 68-70

Beat him enough: after a little time,   [3679]
I'll beat him too.

3. 2. 83-84

Without [his books] he's but a sot, as I am.   [3680]

3. 2. 90-91

[3681]   [You are] a living drollery.

                                              3. 3. 21

[3682]   [Here's] a kind of excellent dumb discourse.

                                              3. 3. 38-39

[3683]   You 'mongst men [are] most unfit to live.

                                              3. 3. 57-58

[3684]   Their great guilt,
         Like poison given to work a great time after,
         Now 'gins to bite the spirits.

                                              3. 3. 104-6

[3685]   The foul lake o'erstunk [your] feet.

                                              4. 1. 183-84

[3686]   I do smell all horse-piss; at which my nose is in great
         indignation.

                                              4. 1. 199-200

[3687]   Foot-licker!

                                              4. 1. 219

[3688]   I do begin to have bloody thoughts.

                                              4. 1. 220-21

[3689]   What do you mean to dote thus on such luggage?

                                              4. 1. 230-31

[3690]   Be turn'd to barnacles, or to apes
         With foreheads villainous low.

                                              4. 1. 248-49

[3691]   Thou, which art but air.

                                              5. 1. 21

You demi-puppets. [3692]

5. 1. 36

Thy brains [3693]
[Are] useless, boil'd within thy skull!

5. 1. 59-60

Most wicked sir, whom to call brother would even infect [3694]
my mouth.

5. 1. 130-31

One of them is a plain fish, and, no doubt, marketable. [3695]

5. 1. 265-66

Be pinch'd to death. [3696]

5. 1. 276

[He] is reeling ripe: where should they [3697]
Find this grand liquor that hath gilded 'em?

5. 1. 279-80

He is as disproportion'd in his manners [3698]
As in his shape.

5. 1. 290-91

What a thrice-double ass [3699]
Was I, to take this drunkard for a god,
And worship this dull fool!

5. 1. 295-97

Timon of Athens

[3700]   [You] glass-fac'd flatterer!

1. 1. 59

[3701]   My estate deserves an heir more rais'd
Than one which holds a trencher.

1. 1. 122-23

[3702]   [You're] but a filthy piece of work.

1. 1. 199

[3703]   Thy mother's of my generation. What's she, if I be a dog?

1. 1. 201-2

[3704]   He that loves to be flattered is worthy o' th' flatterer.

1. 1. 225-26

[3705]   Traffic [commerce] is thy god, and thy god confound thee!

1. 1. 238

[3706]   That there should be small love amongst these sweet
knaves, and all this courtesy! The strain of man's bred
out into baboon and monkey.

1. 1. 248-50

[I'm going to the feast] to see meat fill knaves and wine [3707]
heat fools.

1. 1. 260

Thou art a fool to bid me farewell twice. Shouldst have [3708]
kept one to thyself, for I mean to give thee none.

1. 1. 262-65

I will do nothing at thy bidding. Make thy requests to thy [3709]
friend.

1. 1. 267-68

I will fly, like a dog, the heels o' th' ass. [3710]

1. 1. 271

He's opposite to humanity. [3711]

1. 1. 272

I wonder men dare trust themselves with men. [3712]
Methinks they should invite them without knives:
Good for their meat, and safer for their lives.

1. 2. 43-45

Grant I may never prove so fond, [3713]
To trust man on his oath or bond;
Or a harlot for her weeping,
Or a dog that seems a-sleeping,
Or a keeper with my freedom,
Or my friends, if I should need 'em. Amen.

1. 2. 64-70

Rich men sin, and I eat root. [3714]

1. 2. 71

They are the most needless creatures living, and would [3715]
most resemble sweet instruments hung up in cases.

1. 2. 94-97

[3716] What a sweep of vanity comes this way.

1. 2. 128

[3717] [We] spend our flatteries to drink those men
Upon whose age we void it up again
With poisonous spite and envy.

1. 2. 133-35

[3718] I should fear those that dance before me now
Would one day stamp upon me.

1. 2. 139-40

[3719]   What a coil's here,
Serving of becks and jutting-out of bums!

1. 2. 232-33

[3720] If I should be brib'd too, there would be none left to rail
upon thee, and then thou wouldst sin the faster.

1. 2. 240-42

[3721] [I] must not break my back to heal [your] finger.

2. 1. 24

[3722] Dost dialogue with thy shadow?

2. 2. 56

[3723] Would I had a rod in my mouth, that I might answer thee
profitably.

2. 2. 79-80

[3724] There will little learning die then that day thou art
hang'd.

2. 2. 85-86

[3725] Go, thou wast born a bastard, and thou'lt die a bawd.

2. 2. 87-88

We may account thee a whoremaster and a knave; which [3726]
notwithstanding, thou shalt be no less esteemed.

2. 2. 108-10

[A whoremaster is] a fool in good clothes, and something [3727]
like thee.

2. 2. 112

Thou art not altogether a fool. [3728]

2. 2. 119

[Thou art not] altogether a wise man. As much foolery as [3729]
I have, so much wit thou lack'st.

2. 2. 120-21

These old fellows [3730]
Have their ingratitude in them hereditary;
Their blood is cak'd, 'tis cold, it seldom flows.

2. 2. 218-20

Thou disease of a friend! [3731]

3. 1. 53

Has friendship such a faint and milky heart [3732]
It turns in less than two nights?

3. 1. 54-55

They have all been touch'd and found base metal. [3733]

3. 3. 7

[He] leans wondrously to discontent. [3734]

3. 4. 69

These debts may well be call'd desperate ones, for a [3735]
madman owes 'em.

3. 4. 100-1

[3736] They have e'en put my breath from me, the slaves.
Creditors? Devils!

3. 4. 102-3

[3737] Nothing emboldens sin so much as mercy.

3. 5. 3

[3738] You undergo too strict a paradox,
Striving to make an ugly deed look fair.

3. 5. 24-25

[3739] Your words have took much pains as if they labour'd
To bring manslaughter into form, and set quarrelling
Upon the head of valour.

3. 5. 26-28

[3740] You breathe in vain.

3. 5. 60

[3741] His days are foul and his drink dangerous.

3. 5. 75

[3742] Now the gods keep you old enough, that you may live
Only in bone, that none may look on you!

3. 5. 105-6

[3743] Let no assembly of twenty be without a score of villains.

3. 6. 75

[3744] For these my present friends, as they are to me nothing,
so in nothing bless them, and to nothing are they welcome.

3. 6. 79-81

[3745] You knot of mouth-friends! Smoke and lukewarm water
Is your perfection.

3. 6. 85-86

Live loath'd, and long,   [3746]
Most smiling, smooth, detested parasites,
Courteous destroyers, affable wolves, meek bears,
You fools of fortune, trencher-friends, time's flies,
Cap-and-knee slaves, vapours, and minute-jacks !

3. 6. 89-93

Thou cold sciatica,   [3747]
Cripple our senators, that their limbs may halt
As lamely as their manners!

4. 1. 23-25

Breath infect breath,   [3748]
That their society, as their friendship, may
Be merely poison!

4. 1. 30-32

Nothing I'll bear from thee   [3749]
But nakedness, thou detestable town!

4. 1. 32-33

Leave their false vows with him,   [3750]
Like empty purses pick'd.

4. 2. 11-12

[Thy] learned pate   [3751]
Ducks to the golden fool; all's obliquy.

4. 3. 17-18

There's nothing level in [your] cursed natures   [3752]
But direct villainy. Therefore be abhorr'd
All feasts, societies, and throngs of men!

4. 3. 19-21

Destruction fang mankind!   [3753]

4. 3. 23

[3754] I am Misanthropos, and hate mankind.

4. 3. 54

[3755] I do wish thou wert a dog,
That I might love thee something.

4. 3. 55-56

[3756] Thy lips rot off!

4. 3. 64

[3757] Is this the minion whom the world
Voic'd so regardfully?

4. 3. 82-83

[3758] Be a whore still. They love thee not that use thee.
Give them diseases, leaving with thee their lust.

4. 3. 84-85

[3759]   A counterfeit matron:
It is her habit only that is honest,
Herself's a bawd.

4. 3. 114-16

[3760] Hold up, you sluts, your aprons mountant.

4. 3. 136-37

[3761] Paint [apply cosmetics] till a horse may mire upon your face:
a pox of wrinkles!

4. 3. 149-51

[3762]   Crack the lawyer's voice,
That he may never more false title plead,
Nor sound his quillets shrilly.

4. 3. 155-57

[3763] Make curl'd-pate ruffians bald.

4. 3. 162

[You] unscarr'd braggarts of the war.   [3764]

4. 3. 163

If I hope well, I'll never see thee more.   [3765]

4. 3. 173

Were I like thee I'd throw away myself.   [3766]

4. 3. 221

Thou hast cast away thyself, being like thyself   [3767]
A madman so long, now a fool.

4. 3. 222-23

Thou art a slave, whom Fortune's tender arm   [3768]
With favour never clasp'd, but bred a dog.

4. 3. 252-53

Thy father in spite put stuff   [3769]
To some she-beggar and compounded thee
Poor rogue hereditary.

4. 3. 273-76

If thou hadst not been born the worst of men,   [3770]
Thou hadst been a knave and flatterer.

4. 3. 277-78

Were all the wealth I have shut up in thee,   [3771]
I'ld give thee leave to hang it.

4. 3. 281-82

Mend my company, take away thyself.   [3772]

4. 3. 285

How has the ass broke the wall, that thou art out of the   [3773]
city?

4. 3. 351-52

[3774] When I know not what else to do, I'll see thee again.

4. 3. 355-56

[3775] When there is nothing living but thee, thou shalt be welcome.

4. 3. 357-58

[3776] Thou art the cap of all fools alive.

4. 3. 360

[3777] Would thou wert clean enough to spit upon!

4. 3. 361

[3778] A plague on thee, thou art too bad to curse.

4. 3. 362

[3779] All villains that do stand by thee are pure.

4. 3. 363

[3780] There is no leprosy but what thou speak'st.

4. 3. 364

[3781] I'll beat thee, but I should infect my hands.

4. 3. 366

[3782] Away, thou issue of a mangy dog!

4. 3. 368

[3783] Choler does kill me that thou art alive.

4. 3. 369

[3784] Away, thou tedious rogue, I am sorry I shall lose a stone by thee!

4. 3. 372-73

[3785] Thy back, I prithee.

4. 3. 398

Live, and love thy misery.   [3786]

4. 3. 398

Go, suck the subtle blood o' th' grape,   [3787]
Till the high fever seethe your blood to froth.

4. 3. 432-33

Do villainy, do, since you protest to do't,   [3788]
Like workmen.

4. 3. 437-38

[You've] almost charm'd me from my profession, by per-   [3789]
suading me to it.

4. 3. 453-54

Is not thy kindness subtle, covetous,   [3790]
A usuring kindness, and as rich men deal gifts,
Expecting in return twenty for one?

4. 3. 512-14

Wilt thou whip thine own faults in other men?   [3791]

5. 1. 36-37

Not all the whips of heaven are large enough [for you].   [3792]

5. 1. 59

I am rapt, and cannot cover   [3793]
The monstrous bulk of this ingratitude
With any size of words.

5. 1. 63-65

I thank [you]; and would send [you] back the plague,   [3794]
Could I but catch it for [you].

5. 1. 136-37

Titus Andronicus

[3795] A better head her glorious body fits
Than his that shakes for age and feebleness.

1. 1. 187-88

[3796] Thy years wants wit, thy wits wants edge and manners.

2. 1. 26-27

[3797] Thou dost overween in all.

2. 1. 29

[3798] Are you so desperate grown to threat your friends?

2. 1. 40

[3799] Have your lath glued within your sheath
Till you know better how to handle it.

2. 1. 41-42

[3800] Foul-spoken coward, that thund'rest with thy tongue,
And with thy weapon nothing dar'st perform!

2. 1. 58-59

[3801] This petty brabble will undo us all.

2. 1. 62

Youngling, learn thou to make some meaner choice. [3802]

2. 1. 73

[You are] as hateful as Cocytus' misty mouth. [3803]

2. 3. 236

You recount your sorrows to a stone. [3804]

3. 1. 29

What fool hath added water to the sea, [3805]
Or brought a faggot to bright-burning Troy?

3. 1. 68-69

That kiss is comfortless [3806]
As frozen water to a starved snake.

3. 1. 250-51

Thou map of woe. [3807]

3. 2. 12

I see thou art not for my company. [3808]

3. 2. 58

I will insult on him. [3809]

3. 2. 71

He takes false shadows for true substances. [3810]

3. 2. 80

Now, what a thing it is to be an ass! [3811]

4. 2. 24

Why, what a caterwauling dost thou keep! [3812]

4. 2. 57

[You are] as loathsome as a toad. [3813]

4. 2. 67

[3814] Woe to her chance, and damned her loath'd choice!

4. 2. 78

[3815] Accurs'd the offspring of so foul a fiend!

4. 2. 79

[3816] What, what, ye sanguine, shallow-hearted boys!
Ye white-lim'd walls! ye alehouse painted signs!

4. 2. 97-98

[3817] I blush to think upon this ignomy.

4. 2. 115

[3818] [You] long-tongu'd babbling gossip!

4. 2. 151

[3819] With words more sweet, and yet more dangerous,
Than baits to fish, or honey-stalks to sheep,
When as the one is wounded with the bait,
The other rotted with delicious feed.

4. 4. 90-93

[3820] Say, wall-ey'd slave, whither would'st thou convey
This growing image of thy fiend-like face?

5. 1. 44-45

[3821] Vengeance rot you all!

5. 1. 58

[3822] O most insatiate and luxurious woman!

5. 1. 88

[3823] If there be devils, would I were a devil,
To live and burn in everlasting fire,
So I might have your company in hell,
But to torment you with my bitter tongue!

5. 1. 147-50

Troilus and Cressida

[You are] weaker than a woman's tear,   [3824]
Tamer than sleep, fonder than ignorance,
Less valiant than the virgin in the night,
And skilless as unpractis'd infancy.

                                            1. 1. 9-12

                [Your] spirit of sense [is]   [3825]
Hard as the palm of ploughman.

                                            1. 1. 58-59

He is as valiant as the lion, churlish as the bear, slow as   [3826]
the elephant: a man into whom nature has so crowded
humours that his valour is crushed into folly, his folly
sauced with discretion. There is no man hath a virtue
that he hath not a glimpse of, nor any man an attaint but
he carries some stain of it. He is melancholy without
cause and merry against the hair; he hath the joints of
everything, but everything so out of joint that he is a
gouty Briareus, many hands and no use, or purblind
Argus, all eyes and no sight.

                                            1. 2. 20-31

[3827] He esteems her no more than I esteem an addle egg.

1. 2. 133-34

[3828] If you love an addle egg as well as you love an idle head you would eat chickens i' th' shell.

1. 2. 135-36

[3829] Alas, [your] poor chin, many a wart is richer.

1. 2. 143

[3830] Asses, fools, dolts, chaff and bran, chaff and bran; porridge after meat.

1. 2. 245-46

[3831] Crows and daws, crows and daws!

1. 2. 248

[3832] A drayman, a porter, a very camel.

1. 2. 253

[3833] [He], having his ear full of his airy fame,
Grows dainty of his worth.

1. 3. 144-45

[3834] [You are] a slave whose gall coins slanders like a mint!

1. 3. 193

[3835] Why, this hath not a finger's dignity.

1. 3. 204

[3836] [You] whose grossness little characters sum up!

1. 3. 324-25

[3837] Were not that a botchy core?

2. 1. 6

The plague of Greece upon thee, thou mongrel beef-witted lord! [3838]

2. 1. 12-13

I will beat thee into handsomeness! [3839]

2. 1. 15

I think thy horse will sooner con an oration than thou learn a prayer without book. [3840]

2. 1. 17-18

A red murrain o' thy jade's tricks! [3841]

2. 1. 19-20

Thou art proclaimed fool. [3842]

2. 1. 25

I would thou didst itch from head to foot: and I had the scratching of thee, I would make thee the loathsomest scab in Greece. [3843]

2. 1. 27 29

Cobloaf! [3844]

2. 1. 39

He would pun thee into shivers with his fist, as a sailor breaks a biscuit. [3845]

2. 1. 40-41

Thou stool for a witch! [3846]

2. 1. 44

Thou sodden-witted lord, thou hast no more brain than I have in my elbows: an asinico may tutor thee. [3847]

2. 1. 45-47

[3848] Thou art bought and sold among those of any wit, like a barbarian slave.

2. 1. 48-50

[3849] I will begin at thy heel, and tell what thou art by inches!

2. 1. 50-51

[3850] Thou thing of no bowels thou!

2. 1. 52

[3851] What modicums of wit he utters—his evasions have ears thus long.

2. 1. 70-71

[3852] His pia mater is not worth the ninth part of a sparrow.

2. 1. 73-74

[3853] [He] wears his wit in his belly and his guts in his head.

2. 1. 75-76

[3854] A great deal of your wit lies in your sinews.

2. 1. 100-1

[3855] [You're] a fusty nut with no kernel.

2. 1. 103-4

[3856] [His] wit was mouldy ere your grandsires had nails on their toes.

2. 1. 106-7

[3857] I shall cut out your tongue.
'Tis no matter, I shall speak as much wit as thou after
      wards.

2. 1. 112-14

[3858] I will keep where there is wit stirring, and

Leave the faction of fools.

> 2. 1. 120-21

No marvel though you bite so sharp of reasons, [3859]
You are so empty of them.

> 2. 2. 33-34

Take not that little less than little wit from them that they [3860]
have; which short-armed ignorance itself knows is so
abundant scarce.

> 2. 3. 13-16

If I could a' remembered a gilt counterfeit, thou couldst [3861]
not have slipped out of my contemplation.

> 2. 3. 26-27

The common curse of mankind, folly and ignorance, be [3862]
thine in great revenue: Heaven bless thee from a tutor,
and discipline come not near thee!

> 2. 3. 28-31

If she that lays thee out says thou art a fair corse, I'll be [3863]
sworn and sworn upon't, she never shrouded any but
lazars.

> 2. 3. 32-35

Why are you a fool? [3864]
Make that demand of the Creator, it suffices me thou art.

> 2. 3. 68-70

You may call it melancholy if you will favour the man, but [3865]
by my head 'tis pride.

> 2. 3. 89-91

We think him over-proud [3866]
And under-honest, in self-assumption greater

Than in the note of judgment.

2. 3. 125-27

[3867] I do hate a proud man as I do hate the engendering of toads.

2. 3. 160-61

[3868] He is so plaguy proud that the death-tokens of it
Cry 'No Recovery.'

2. 3. 178-79

[3869] That were to enlard his fat-already pride.

2. 3. 196

[3870] A paltry, insolent fellow!

2. 3. 209

[3871] He will be the physician that should be the patient.

2. 3. 214-15

[3872] I will knead him, I'll make him supple.

2. 3. 222

[3873] Friend, we understand not one another: I am too courtly, and thou art too cunning.

3. 1. 26-27

[3874] There's a stewed phrase indeed!

3. 1. 40-41

[3875] Words pay no debts.

3. 2. 55

[3876] What folly I commit, I dedicate to you.

3. 2. 101-2

Lay negligent and loose regard upon him. [3877]

3. 3. 41

[You] great-siz'd monster of ingratitude! [3878]

3. 3. 147

[You] hang [3879]
Quite out of fashion, like a rusty mail
In monumental mockery.

3. 3. 151-53

He is so prophetically proud of an heroical cudgelling that [3880]
he raves in saying nothing.

3. 3. 247-48

[Wit] lies as coldly in him as fire in a flint, which will not [3881]
show without knocking.

3. 3. 255-57

He's grown a very land-fish, languageless, a monster. [3882]

3. 3. 262-63

Would the fountain of your mind were clear again, that I [3883]
might water an ass at it.

3. 3. 308-9

I had rather be a tick in a sheep than such a valiant [3884]
ignorance.

3. 3. 309-10

We know each other well. [3885]
We do, and long to know each other worse.

4. 1. 31-32

Since she could speak, [3886]
She hath not given so many good words breath.

4. 1. 73-74

[3887] A bugbear take him!

4. 2. 33

[3888] She is as far high-soaring o'er thy praises
As thou unworthy to be call'd her servant.

4. 4. 122-23

[3889] The kiss you take is better than you give:
Therefore, no kiss.

4. 5. 38-39

[3890]   Her wanton spirits look out
At every joint and motive of her body.

4. 5. 56-57

[3891]   Set them down
For sluttish spoils of opportunity
And daughters of the game.

4. 5. 61-63

[3892] It would discredit the blest gods, proud man,
To answer such a question.

4. 5. 246-47

[3893] To such as boasting show their scars
A mock is due.

4. 5. 289-90

[3894] Thou crusty botch of nature!

5. 1. 5

[3895] Idol of idiot-worshippers!

5. 1. 7

[3896] Thou full dish of fool!

5. 1. 9

I profit not by thy talk.

[3897]

5. 1. 13

Now the rotten diseases of the south, the guts-griping, ruptures, catarrhs, loads o' gravel i'th'back, lethargies, cold palsies, raw eyes, dirt-rotten livers, whissing lungs, bladders full of impostume, sciaticas, lime-kilns i'th'palm, incurable bone-ache, and the rivelled fee-simple of the tetter, take and take again such preposterous discoveries!

[3898]

5. 1. 16-23

Thou damnable box of envy, thou.

[3899]

5. 1. 24

You ruinous butt, you whoreson indistinguishable cur!

[3900]

5. 1. 27-28

Thou idle immaterial skein of sleave silk, thou green sarsenet flap for a sore eye, thou tassel of a prodigal's purse, thou: ah, how the poor world is pestered with such water-flies, diminutives of nature!

[3901]

5. 1. 29-33

Finch egg!

[3902]

5. 1. 35

With too much blood and too little brain these two may run mad.

[3903]

5. 1. 47-48

He has not so much brain as ear-wax.

[3904]

5. 1. 51-52

[He's] the primitive statue and oblique memorial of cuck-olds.

[3905]

5. 1. 54-55

[3906] To be a dog, a mule, a cat, a fitchook, a toad, a lizard, an owl, a puttock, or a herring without a roe, I would not care; but to be [him] I would conspire against destiny. Ask me not what I would be, if I were not [myself]; for I care not to be the louse of a lazar, so I were not [him].

5. 1. 60-66

[3907] Sweet sink, sweet sewer!

5. 1. 75-76

[3908] I will no more trust him when he leers then I will a serpent when he hisses.

5. 2. 88-89

[3909] Nothing but lechery: all incontinent varlets!

5. 1. 97

[3910] Any man may sing her, if he can take her clef: she's noted.

5. 2. 10-11

[3911] How the devil Luxury, with his fat rump and potato finger, tickles these together!

5. 2. 55-56

[3912] If beauty have a soul, this is not she.

5. 2. 137

[3913] [You] stale old mouse-eaten dry cheese!

5. 4. 10-11

[3914] That same dog-fox is not proved worth a blackberry.

5. 4. 11-12

[3915] There they fly, or die, like scaled sculls
Before the belching whale.

5. 5. 22-23

Bastard begot, bastard instructed, bastard in mind, [3916]
bastard in valour, in everything illegitimate.

                                  5. 7. 17-18

               Thou great-siz'd coward, [3917]
No space of earth shall sunder our two hates:
I'll haunt thee like a wicked conscience still,
That mouldeth goblins swift as frenzy's thoughts.

                                  5. 10. 26-29

Hence, broker-lackey! Ignomy and shame [3918]
Pursue thy life, and live aye with thy name!

                                  5. 10. 33-34

[You] brethren and sisters of the hold-door trade! [3919]

                                  5. 10. 52

Twelfth Night

[3920] What great ones do, the less will prattle of.

1. 2. 33

[3921] Let them hang themselves in their own straps.

1. 3. 12-13

[3922] Besides that he's a fool, he's a great quarreller; and but that he hath the gift of a coward to allay the gust he hath in quarrelling, 'tis thought among the prudent he would quickly have the gift of a grave.

1. 3. 29-33

[3923] He's a coward and a coistrel that will not drink to [her] till his brains turn o' th' toe, like a parish top.

1. 3. 40-42

[3924] Fair lady, do you think you have fools in hand?

1. 3. 63-64

[3925] I am not such an ass but I can keep my hand dry.

1. 3. 73-74

Methinks sometimes [you] have no more wit than a [3926]
Christian or an ordinary man has: but [you are] a great
eater of beef, and I believe that does harm to [your] wit.
1. 3. 82-85

[Your hair] hangs like flax on a distaff; and I hope to see a [3927]
housewife take thee between her legs, and spin it off.
1. 3. 99-101

[You are] a fellow o' th' strangest mind i' th' world. [3928]
1. 3. 110-11

Well, God give them wisdom that have it; and those that [3929]
are fools, let them use their talents.
1. 5. 14-15

Many a good hanging prevents a bad marriage. [3930]
1. 5. 19

I am resolved on two points. [3931]
That if one break, the other will hold: or if both break,
your gaskins fall.
1. 5. 22-24

Go to, y'are a dry fool: I'll no more of you. Besides, you [3932]
grow dishonest.
1. 5. 38-39

The lady bade take away the fool, therefore I say again, [3933]
take her away.
1. 5. 50-51

[He] will be sworn that I am no fox, but he will not pass [3934]
his word for twopence that you are no fool.
1. 5. 78-79

[3935] Unless you laugh and minister occasion to him, he is gagged.

1. 5. 85-86

[3936] I take these wise men, that crow so at these set kind of fools, no better than the fools' zanies.

1. 5. 86-88

[3937] O, you are sick of self-love and taste with a distempered appetite.

1. 5. 89-90

[3938] To be generous, guiltless, and of free disposition, is to take those things for bird-bolts that you deem cannon-bullets.

1. 5. 90-93

[3939] He speaks nothing but madman.

1. 5. 106-7

[3940] How your fooling grows old, and people dislike it.

1. 5. 111-12

[3941] One of thy kin has a most weak pia mater.

1. 5. 115-16

[3942] A plague o' these pickle-herring!

1. 5. 121-22

[3943] How have you come so early by this lethargy!

1. 5. 124-25

[3944] Not yet old enough for a man, nor young enough for a boy: as a squash is before 'tis a peascod, or a codling when 'tis almost an apple. 'Tis with him in standing water, between boy and man.

1. 5. 158-61

[I] allowed your approach rather to wonder at you than to hear you.   [3945]

> 1. 5. 199-200

If you be mad, be gone: if you have reason, be brief.   [3946]

> 1. 5. 200-1

The rudeness that hath appeared in me have I learned from my entertainment.   [3947]

> 1. 5. 217-18

Lady, you are the cruell'st she alive.   [3948]

> 1. 5. 244

Love make his heart of flint that you shall love, And let your fervour be plac'd in contempt.   [3949]

> 1. 5. 290-92

Pardon me, sir, your bad entertainment.   [3950]

> 2. 1. 32

A false conclusion: I hate it as an unfilled can.   [3951]

> 2. 3. 6

Th'art a scholar; let us therefore eat and drink.   [3952]

> 2. 3. 13

Welcome, ass.   [3953]

> 2. 3. 18

What a caterwauling do you keep here?   [3954]

> 2. 3. 73

Have you no wit, manners, nor honesty, but to gabble like tinkers at this time of night?   [3955]

> 2. 3. 88-89

[3956] Is there no respect of place, persons, nor time in you?

2. 3. 92-93

[3957] Though she harbours you as her kinsman, she's nothing allied to your disorders.

2. 3. 95-97

[3958] If you can separate yourself and your misdemeanours, you are welcome to the house: if not, she is very willing to bid you farewell.

2. 3. 98-101

[3959] If I do not gull him into a nayword, and make him a common recreation, do not think I have wit enough to lie straight in my bed.

2. 3. 135-138

[3960] The devil a Puritan that he is, or any thing constantly, but a time-pleaser, an affectioned ass, that cons state without book, and utters it by great swarths: the best persuaded of himself, so crammed (as he thinks) with excellencies, that it is his grounds of faith that all that look on him love him.

2. 3. 146-52

[3961] On that vice in him will my revenge find notable cause to work.

2. 3. 152-53

[3962] Your horse now would make him an ass.

2. 3. 169

[3963] Give me now leave to leave thee.

2. 4. 72

[3964] Now the melancholy god protect thee, and the tailor make

thy doublet of changeable taffeta, for thy mind is a very
opal.

> 2. 4. 73-75

I would have men of such constancy put to sea, that their [3965]
business might be everything, and their intent everywhere, for that's it that always makes a good voyage of
nothing.

> 2. 4. 75-78

If I lose a scruple of this sport, let me be boiled to death [3966]
with melancholy.

> 2. 5. 2-3

He has been yonder i' the sun practising behaviour to his [3967]
own shadow.

> 2. 5. 16-17

Observe him, for the love of mockery. [3968]

> 2. 5. 18-19

Here comes the trout that must be caught with tickling. [3969]

> 2. 5. 21-22

Contemplation makes a rare turkey-cock of him: how he [3970]
jets under his advanced plumes!

> 2. 5. 30-32

Shall this fellow live? [3971]

> 2. 5. 63

Now is the woodcock near the gin. [3972]

> 2. 5. 84

What dish o' poison has she dressed him! [3973]

> 2. 5. 114

[3974] The cur is excellent at faults.

2. 5. 128-29

[3975] [If] you had any eye behind you, you might see more detraction at your heels than fortunes before you.

2. 5. 136-38

[3976] Let me see thee a steward still, the fellow of servants, and not worthy to touch Fortune's fingers.

2. 5. 155-57

[3977] I will wash off gross acquaintance.

2. 5. 162-63

[3978] It cannot but turn him into a notable contempt.

2. 5. 203-4

[3979] They that dally nicely with words may quickly make them wanton.

3. 1. 14-15

[3980] I do care for something; but in my conscience, sir, I do not care for you: if that be to care for nothing, sir, I would it would make you invisible.

3. 1. 28-31

[3981] She will keep no fool, sir, till she be married, and fools are as like husbands as pilchards are to herrings, the husband's the bigger.

3. 1. 33-36

[3982] [You] corrupter of words!

3. 1. 37

[3983] Foolery, sir, does walk about the orb like the sun, it shines everywhere.

3. 1. 39-40

Now Jove, in his next commodity of hair, send thee a   [3984]
beard!

3. 1. 45 46

Taste your legs, sir, put them to motion.   [3985]

3. 1. 79

Most excellent accomplished lady, the heavens rain   [3986]
odours on you!

3. 1. 86-87

Thy reason, dear venom, give thy reason.   [3987]

3. 2. 2

Awake your dormouse valour, put fire in your heart, and   [3988]
brimstone in your liver!

3. 2. 17-19

With some excellent jests, fire-new from the mint, you   [3989]
should have banged the youth into dumbness.

3. 2. 20-22

This was looked for at your hand, and this was balked: [3990]
the double gilt of this opportunity you let time wash off,
and you are now sailed into the north of my lady's opinion, where you will hang like an icicle on a Dutchman's
beard.

3. 2. 22-31

If he were opened and you find so much blood in his liver   [3991]
as will clog the foot of a flea, I'll eat the rest of th'
anatomy.

3. 2. 58-61

Yond gull is turned heathen, a very renegado; for there is   [3992]
no Christian that means to be saved by believing rightly

can ever believe such impossible passages of grossness.

3. 2. 66-69

[3993] I have dogged him like his murderer.

3. 2. 73-74

[3994] I can hardly forbear hurling things at him.

3. 2. 78-79

[3995] The man is tainted in's wits.

3. 4. 13

[3996] Why appear you with this ridiculous boldness?

3. 4. 36

[3997] This is very midsummer madness.

3. 4. 55

[3998] Go off, I discard you. Let me enjoy my private.

3. 4. 90-91

[3999] Lo, how hollow the fiend speaks within him!

3. 4. 92

[4000] Go hang yourselves all: you are idle, shallow things, I am not of your element.

3. 4. 124-25

[4001] If this were played upon a stage now, I could condemn it as an improbable fiction.

3. 4. 128-29

[4002] His very genius hath taken the infection of the device, man.

3. 4. 130-31

More matter for a May morning! [4003]

3. 4. 144

Youth, whatsoever thou art, thou art but a scurvy fellow. [4004]

3. 4. 149-50

A terrible oath, with a swaggering accent sharply twanged [4005]
off, gives manhood more approbation than ever proof
itself would have earned him.

3. 4. 180-83

This letter, being so excellently ignorant, will breed no [4006]
terror in the youth: he will find it comes from a clodpole.

3. 4. 189-91

This will so fright them both that they will kill one an- [4007]
other by the look, like cockatrices.

3. 4. 196-98

I have said too much unto a heart of stone. [4008]

3. 4. 203

Such a headstrong potent fault it is, [4009]
That it but mocks reproof.

3. 4. 206-7

A fiend like thee might bear my soul to hell. [4010]

3. 4. 219

This is as uncivil as strange. [4011]

3. 4. 257

What manner of man is he? [4012]
Nothing of that wonderful promise, to read him by his
form.

3. 4. 267-69

[4013] I have not seen such a Firago.

3. 4. 278-79

[4014] I hate ingratitude more in a man
Than lying, vainness, babbling drunkenness,
Or any taint of vice whose strong corruption
Inhabits our frail blood.

3. 4. 363-66

[4015] [You are] a very dishonest paltry boy, and more a coward
than a hare.

3. 4. 395-96

[4016] [You are] a coward, a most devout coward, religious in it.

3. 4. 399

[4017] Vent thy folly somewhere else.

4. 1. 10

[4018] I would not be in some of your coats for twopence.

4. 1. 29-30

[4019]   Ungracious wretch,
Fit for the mountains and the barbarous caves,
Where manners ne'er were preach'd! Out of my sight!

4. 1. 46-48

[4020] Rudesby, be gone!

4. 1. 50

[4021]   How many fruitless pranks
This ruffian hath botch'd up.

4. 1. 54-55

[4022] The knave counterfeits well: a good knave.

4. 2. 20

Out, hyperbolical fiend! [4023]

4. 2. 26

Fie, thou dishonest Satan! (I call thee by the most modest [4024]
terms, for I am one of those gentle ones that will use the
devil himself with courtesy.)

4. 2. 32-34

This house is as dark as ignorance, though ignorance [4025]
were as dark as hell.

4. 2. 46-47

Leave thy vain bibble babble. [4026]

4. 2. 100

I'll ne'er believe a madman till I see his brains. [4027]

4. 2. 120-21

They praise you, and make an ass of you. Now your foes [4028]
tell you plainly you are an ass: so that by your foes, sir,
you profit in the knowledge of yourself, and by your
friends you are abused.

5. 1. 10-19

[This] is as fat and fulsome to mine ear [4029]
As howling after music.

5. 1. 107-8

Live you the marble-breasted tyrant still. [4030]

5. 1. 122

[You are] an ass-head, and a coxcomb, and a knave, a [4031]
thin-faced knave, a gull.

5. 1. 204-5

The Two Gentlemen of Verona

[4032] Home-keeping youth have ever homely wits.

1. 1. 2

[4033] He that is so yoked by a fool
Methinks should not be chronicled for wise.

1. 1. 40-41

[4034] Wherefore waste I time to counsel thee
That art a votary to fond desire?

1. 1. 51-52

[4035] Here's too small a pasture for such store of muttons.

1. 1. 98

[4036] Beshrew me, but you have a quick wit.
And yet it cannot overtake your slow purse.

1. 1. 120-21

[4037] [You] worthless post!

1. 1. 147

[4038] Dare you presume to harbour wanton lines?

To whisper, and conspire against my youth?

1. 2. 42-43

Kill your stomach on your meat,   [4039]
And not upon your maid.

1. 2. 68-69

You, minion, are too saucy.   [4040]

1. 2. 92

This babble shall not henceforth trouble me.   [4041]

1. 2. 99

I throw thy name against the bruising stones.   [4042]

1. 2. 112

[You are] the sourest-natured dog that lives.   [4043]

2. 3. 5-6

He is a stone, a very pebble stone.   [4044]

2. 3. 9-10

He is a kind of chameleon.   [4045]
That hath more mind to feed on your blood than live in
        your air.

2. 4. 25-26

If you spend word for word with me, I shall make your wit   [4046]
bankrupt.

2. 4. 37-38

What braggardism is this?   [4047]

2. 4. 159

                She is peevish, sullen, froward,   [4048]
Proud, disobedient, stubborn, lacking duty.

3. 1. 68-69

[4049] That man that hath a tongue, I say is no man,
If with his tongue he cannot win a woman.

3. 1. 104-5

[4050] I have the wit to think my master is a kind of a knave.

3. 1. 261-62

[4051] O illiterate loiterer!

3. 1. 290

[4052] [Yours are] 'bastard virtues'; that indeed know not their fathers, and therefore have no names.

3. 1. 312-14

[4053] She hath more hair than wit, and more faults than hairs, and more wealth than faults.

3. 1. 344-45

[4054] She is lumpish, heavy, melancholy.

3. 2. 62

[4055] We detest such vile base practices.

4. 1. 73

[4056] Thou subtle, perjur'd, false, disloyal man!

4. 2. 92

[4057] When didst thou see me heave up my leg, and make water against a gentlewoman's farthingale? Didst thou ever see me do such a trick?

4. 4. 37-39

[4058] How now, you whoreson peasant, Where have you been these two days loitering?

4. 4. 43-44

Thou friend of an ill fashion!   [4059]

5. 4. 61

How oft hast thou with perjury cleft the root!   [4060]

5. 4. 102

            It is the lesser blot modesty finds,   [4061]
Women to change their shapes, than men their minds.

5. 4. 107-8

I dare thee but to breathe upon my love.   [4062]

5. 4. 129

I hold him but a fool that will endanger   [4063]
His body for a girl that loves him not.

5. 4. 131-32

Degenerate and base art thou.   [4064]

5. 4. 134

The Two Noble Kinsmen

[4065]   O fan
From me the witless chaff of such a writer!

Prologue 18-19

[4066] [You are] full of bread and sloth.

1. 1. 158-59

[4067] What strange ruins may we perceive walking [here]?

1. 2. 13-15

[4068]   Why am I bound
By any generous bond to follow him
Follows his tailor?

1. 2. 49-51

[4069] Let the blood of mine that's sib to him be sucked
From me with leeches.

1. 2. 71-72

[4070] [You are] leaden-footed!

1. 2. 84

Small winds shake him. [4071]

1. 2. 88

I must no more believe thee in this point [4072]
Than I will trust a sickly appetite,
That loathes even as it longs.

1. 3. 87-90

Let 'em suffer the gall of hazard. [4073]

2. 2. 65-66

That was a fair boy, certain, but a fool [4074]
To love himself.

2. 2. 120-21

Men are mad things. [4075]

2. 2. 126

Let me deal coldly with you. [4076]

2. 2. 186

You play the child extremely. [4077]

2. 2. 206

Thou art baser than a cutpurse. [4078]

2. 2. 213

Thou dar'st not, fool, thou canst not, thou art feeble. [4079]

2. 2. 216

I shall live [4080]
To knock thy brains out.

2. 2. 220-21

Thou bring'st such pelting scurvy news continually, [4081]
Thou art not worthy life.

2. 2. 268-69

[4082] To marry him is hopeless,
To be his whore is witless.

2. 4. 4-5

[4083]   I'll proclaim him,
And to his face, no man.

2. 6. 30-31

[4084] [You are] a very thief in love, a chaffy lord,
Not worth the name of villain.

3. 1. 41-42

[4085]   You might as well
Speak this and act it in your glass as to
His ear which now disdains you.

3. 1. 69-71

[4086]   Most certain
You love me not; be rough with me, and pour
This oil out of your language.

3. 1. 101-3

[4087] Thy best props are warped!

3. 2. 32

[4088] No more of these vain parleys.

3. 3. 10

[4089] Fool, away with this strained mirth.

3. 3. 43-44

[4090] Fie, fie, what tediosity and disinsanity is here among ye!

3. 5. 1-2

[4091] My friend, carry your tail without offence
Or scandal to the ladies.

3. 5. 31-32

[Your] business is become a nullity.   [4092]

3. 5. 51

There's a dainty madwoman as mad as a March hare.   [4093]

3. 5. 69-70

Give me your hand. I can tell your fortune.   [4094]
You are a fool.

3. 5. 74-75

[You] lay fatting like a swine to fight.   [4095]

3. 6. 12

That face of yours   [4096]
Will bear the curses else of after ages.

3. 6. 186-87

She sung much, but no sense.   [4097]

4. 1. 66

They must all be gelt for musicians.   [4098]

4. 1. 132

She's lost past all cure.   [4099]

4. 1. 137-38

[He] is but his foil, to him a mere dull shadow.   [4100]

4. 2. 26

[You] have lied so lewdly   [4101]
That women ought to beat [you].

4. 2. 35-36

Be put in a cauldron of lead and usurers' grease,   [4102]
amongst a whole million of cutpurses, and there boil like
a gammon of bacon that will never be enough.

4. 3. 33-35

[4103] How her brain coins!

4. 3. 36

[4104] [You] shall stand in fire up to the navel and in ice up to th' heart, and there th' offending part burns and the deceiving part freezes.

4. 3. 38-40

[4105] Believe me, one would marry a leprous witch to be rid on't.

4. 3. 42-43

[4106] I think she has a perturbed mind, which I cannot minister to.

4. 3. 55-56

[4107] They are now in a most extravagant vagary.

4. 3. 67-68

[4108] Him I do not love that tells close offices
The foulest way, nor names concealments in
The boldest language.

5. 1. 122-24

[4109] [You] abandoner of revels, mute contemplative!

5. 1. 138

[4110] Those darker humours [do] stick misbecomingly.

5. 3. 53-54

[4111] Pig-like he whines.

5. 4. 69

The Winter's Tale

We'll thwack him hence with distaffs.   [4112]

1. 2. 37

You would seek t' unsphere the stars with oaths.   [4113]

1. 2. 48

What! hast smutch'd thy nose?   [4114]

1. 2. 121

With what's unreal thou coactive art.   [4115]

1. 2. 141

Many a man there is (even at this present,   [4116]
Now, while I speak this) holds his wife by th' arm,
That little thinks she has been sluic'd in 's absence
And his pond fish'd by his next neighbour, by
Sir Smile, his neighbour.

1. 2. 192-96

        Should all despair   [4117]
That have revolted wives, the tenth of mankind
Would hang themselves.

1. 2. 198-200

[4118] [Here are] some severals of head-piece extraordinary.

1. 2. 226-27

[4119] Lower messes perchance are to this business purblind?

1. 2. 227-28

[4120]   Thou art not honest: or,
If thou inclin'st that way, thou art a coward,
Which hoxes honesty behind, restraining
From course requir'd: or else thou must be counted
A servant grafted in my serious trust,
And therein negligent; or else a fool,
That seest a game play'd home, the rich stake drawn,
And tak'st it all for jest.

1. 2. 242-49

[4121]   Your eye-glass
Is thicker than a cuckold's horn.

1. 2. 268-69

[4122] To a vision so apparent rumour cannot be mute.

1. 2. 270-71

[4123] Cogitation resides not in that man that does not think.

1. 2. 271-72

[4124] [Your] wife is slippery.

1. 2. 273

[4125] My wife's a hobby-horse.

1. 2. 276

[4126]   [She] deserves a name
As rank as any flax-wench that puts to
Before her troth-plight.

1. 2. 276-78

You never spoke what did become you less than this.   [4127]

1. 2. 282-83

           Be cur'd   [4128]
Of this diseas'd opinion, and betimes,
For 'tis most dangerous.

1. 2. 296-98

           I hate thee,   [4129]
Pronounce thee a gross lout, a mindless slave,
Or else a hovering temporizer that
Canst with thine eyes at once see good and evil,
Inclining to them both.

1. 2. 300-4

           Were my wife's liver   [4130]
Infected, as her life, she would not live
The running of one glass.

1. 2. 304 6

Go rot!   [4131]

1. 2. 324

This is strange: methinks   [4132]
My favour here begins to warp.

1. 2. 364-65

A lip of much contempt speeds from me.   [4133]

1. 2. 373

Be intelligent to me.   [4134]

1. 2. 378

[You are] hated too, worse than the great'st infection that   [4135]
e'er was heard or read!

1. 2. 423-24

[4136] She is spread of late into a goodly bulk.

2. 1. 19-20

[4137] The shrug, the hum or ha, these petty brands
That calumny doth use.

2. 1. 71-72

[4138] O thou thing!

2. 1. 82

[4139] She's a bed-swerver, even as bad as
Those that vulgars give bold'st titles.

2. 1. 92-94

[4140] You smell this business with a sense as cold as is a dead
man's nose.

2. 1. 151-52

[4141] We need no grave to bury honesty:
There's not a grain of it the face to sweeten
Of the whole dungy earth.

2. 1. 155-57

[4142] Either thou art most ignorant by age, or thou wert born a
fool.

2. 1. 173-74

[4143] A mankind witch!

2. 3. 67

[4144] I am no less honest than you are mad.

2. 3. 69-71

[4145] The root of his opinion, is rotten
As ever oak or stone was sound.

2. 3. 89-90

[She is] a callat   [4146]
Of boundless tongue, who late hath beat her husband,
And now baits me!

                                   2. 3. 90-92

[You are] not able to produce more accusation   [4147]
Than your own weak-hing'd fancy.

                                   2. 3. 117-18

[You are] a feather for each wind that blows.   [4148]
                                   2. 3. 153

Female bastard!   [4149]
                                   2. 3. 174

                [Thy jealousies are]   [4150]
Fancies too weak for boys, too green and idle
For girls of nine.

                                   3. 2. 181-82

Thy by-gone fooleries were but spices of [thy tyranny].   [4151]
                                   3. 2. 184

                A thousand knees   [4152]
Ten thousand years together, naked, fasting,
Upon a barren mountain, and still winter
In storm perpetual, could not move the gods
To look that way thou wert.

                                   3. 2. 210-14

This place is famous for the creatures of prey that keep   [4153]
upon't.

                                   3. 3. 12-13

I would there were no age between ten and three-and-   [4154]
twenty, or that youth would sleep out the rest; for there is
nothing in the between but getting wenches with child,

wronging the ancientry, steeling, fighting.

3. 3. 59-63

[4155] Would any but these boiled-brains hunt this weather?

3. 3. 63-65

[4156] This has been some stair-work, some trunk-work, some behind-door-work.

3. 3. 73-75

[4157] If thou'lt see a thing to talk on when thou art dead and rotten, come hither.

3. 3. 80-81

[4158] [You] snapper-up of unconsidered trifles.

4. 3. 26

[4159] Thou hast need of more rags to lay on thee.

4. 3. 54-55

[4160] [This is] a fellow, sir, that I have known to go about with troll-my-dames.

4. 3. 84-85

[4161] Having flown over many knavish professions, he settled only in rogue.

4. 3. 95-96

[4162] If you had but looked big and spit at him, he'd have run.

4. 3. 103

[4163] [You are] so lean that blasts of January
Would blow you through and through.

4. 4. 111-12

[4164] Good sooth, she is the queen of curds and cream.

4. 4. 160-61

[You] stretch-mouthed rascal!   [4165]

4. 4. 198

Is there no manners left among maids?   [4166]

4. 4. 244

She longed to eat adders' heads and toads carbonadoed.   [4167]

4. 4. 265-66

Why should I carry lies abroad?   [4168]

4. 4. 272

A gallimaufry of gambols!   [4169]

4. 4. 329

Here has been too much homely foolery already.   [4170]

4. 4. 333-34

Thou art too base to be a acknowledg'd.   [4171]

4. 4. 419-20

Thou fresh piece of excellent witchcraft!   [4172]

4. 4. 423-24

To have an open ear, a quick eye, and a nimble hand, is   [4173]
necessary for a cut-purse; a good nose is requisite also,
to smell out work for the other senses.

4. 4. 670-73

I see this is the time that the unjust man doth thrive.   [4174]

4. 4. 673-74

Though [he] is not naturally honest, [he] is so sometimes   [4175]
by chance.

4. 4. 712-13

[4176] [You] pedlar's excrement.

4. 4. 713-14

[4177] You are rough and hairy.

4. 4. 722

[4178] Receives not thy nose court-odour from me? reflect I not on thy baseness, court-contempt?

4. 4. 732-34

[4179] How blessed are we that are not simple men!
Yet nature might have made me as these are;
Therefore I will not disdain.

4. 4. 746-48

[4180] His garments are rich, but he wears them not handsomely.

4. 4. 750-51

[4181] The curses he shall have, the tortures he shall feel, will break the back of man, the heart of monster.

4. 4. 769-71

[4182] [You are] an old sheep-whistling rogue.

4. 4. 777

[4183] What talk we of these traitorly rascals, whose miseries are to be smiled at, their offences being so capital?

4. 4. 793-95

[4184] Though authority be a stubborn bear, yet he is oft led by the nose with gold.

4. 4. 803-4

[4185] Here come those I have done good to against my will.

5. 2. 124-25

[You are] boors and franklins.

[4186]

5. 2. 159-60

I know thou art no tall fellow of thy hands and that thou
wilt be drunk.

[4187]

5. 2. 165-66

We honour you with trouble.

[4188]

5. 3. 9

Does not the stone rebuke [you]
For being more stone than it?

[4189]

5. 3. 37-38

[She] should be hooted at like an old tale.

[4190]

5. 3. 116-17

PART III

READY INSULTS
FOR PARTICULAR OCCASIONS

SHAKESPEARE'S insults display astonishing variety because he fashioned them for particular characters. Follow his example. When some coxcomb arouses your scorn, you'll want to choose an aiming point. Fire at the base extremes of his behaviour that make him who he is.

Sweet smoke of rhetoric, I shoot thee at the swain!

This brief and useful index equips you for these extremes of humanness that go off the edge into realms of offensiveness. You can find words here for those who curdle one of the five senses or fail in some principal virtue. And in case your antagonist owns no single exaggerated quality, we have included jibes against those who are so vilely ordinary that drowsiness itself mocks them.

EYE-CATCHERS
THE ROTUND

[What a] mountain of mad flesh!

The Comedy of Errors   4. 4. 152

[He] sweats to death,
And lards the lean earth as he walks along.

Henry IV, part 1 2. 2. 103-4

Why dost thou converse with that trunk of humours, that bolting-hutch of beastliness, that swollen parcel of dropsies, that huge bombard of sack, that stuffed cloak-bag of guts, that roasted Manningtree ox with the pudding in his belly, that reverend Vice, that grey Iniquity, that father Ruffian, that Vanity in years?

Henry IV, part 1 2. 4. 442-49

If [your girdle should break], how would thy guts fall about thy knees!

Henry IV, part 1 3. 3. 151-52

Make less thy body hence, and more thy grace.

Henry IV, part 2 5. 5. 52

Such a keech can with his very bulk
Take up the rays o'th'beneficial sun,
And keep it from the earth.

Henry VIII 1. 1. 55-57

What tempest, I trow, threw this whale, with so many tuns of oil in his belly, ashore?

The Merry Wives of Windsor 2. 1. 61-63

THE SPINDLING

[You are] a hungry lean-fac'd villain;
A mere anatomy, a mountebank,
A thread-bare juggler and a fortune-teller,
A needy-hollow-ey'd-sharp-looking-wretch,
A living dead man.

The Comedy of Errors 5. 1. 238-42

You starvelling, you eel-skin, you dried neat's-tongue, you bull's-pizzle, you stock-fish—O for breath to utter what is like thee!—you tailor's-yard, you sheath, you bow-case, you vile standing tuck!

Henry IV, part 1   2. 4. 240-44

[You are] a man made after supper of a cheese-paring.

Henry IV, part 2   3. 2. 303-4

You might have thrust him and all his apparel into an eel-skin.

Henry IV, part 2   3. 2. 319-20

THE STRIKING

Do thou amend thy face, and I'll amend my life.

Henry IV, part 1 3. 3. 23

I never see thy face but I think upon hell-fire.

Henry IV, part 1   3. 3. 29-30

[Your] face is Lucifer's privy kitchen, where he doth nothing but roast malt-worms.

Henry IV, part 2   2. 4. 330-31

[Your] face is not worth sunburning.

Henry V   5. 2. 150

Old age, that ill layer-up of beauty, can do no more spoil upon [your] face.

Henry V   5. 2. 242-43

[You are] the scarecrow that affrights our children so.

Henry VI, part 1 1. 4. 42

Sell your face for five pence and 'tis dear.

King John 1. 1. 153

I have seen better faces in my time
Than stands on any shoulder that I see
Before me at this instant.

King Lear 2. 2. 94-96

[Your] horrid image doth unfix my hair.

Macbeth 1. 3. 135

Approach the chamber, and destroy your sight with a
new Gorgon.

Macbeth 2. 3. 72-73

FOUL EMANATIONS

ODOURS

Foh! Prithee stand away. A paper from Fortune's closestool!

All's Well That Ends Well 5. 2. 16-17

His celestial breath was sulphurous to smell.

Cymbeline 5. 4. 114-15

They have marvellous foul linen.

Henry V 5. 1. 31-32

His breath stinks with eating toasted cheese.

Henry VI, part 2 4. 7. 10-11

The rabblement hooted, and clapp'd their chapped

hands, and threw up their sweaty night-caps, and uttered such a deal of stinking breath that it had, almost,
choked [us].

Julius Caesar 1. 2. 240-44

I durst not laugh, for fear of opening my lips and receiving the bad air [from your stinking breath].

Julius Caesar 1. 2. 246-47

[You have] a blasting and a scandalous breath.

Measure for Measure 5. 1. 125

Then did the sun on dunghill shine.

The Merry Wives of Windsor 1. 3. 59

[This is] the rankest compound of villainous smell that
ever offended nostril.

The Merry Wives of Windsor 3. 5. 82-84

If her breath were as terrible as her terminations, there
were no living near her, she would infect to the North
Star.

Much Ado About Nothing 2. 1. 232-34

Art thou the slave that with thy breath hast kill'd?

Much Ado About Nothing 5. 1. 257

I do smell all horse-piss; at which my nose is in great
indignation.

The Tempest 4. 1. 199-200

IMPOLITE SOUNDS

Three times was his nose discharg'd against me; he

stands there like a mortar-piece to blow us.

Henry VIII 5. 3. 43-45

His forward voice, now, is to speak well of his friend; his backward voice is to utter foul speeches and to detract.

The Tempest 2. 2. 91-94

Doth thy other mouth call me?

The Tempest 2. 2. 98

OILINESS

She's the kitchen wench, and all grease, and I know not what use to put her to but to make a lamp of her, and run from her by her own light.

The Comedy of Errors 3. 2. 93-96

I warrant her rags and the tallow in them will burn a Poland winter.

The Comedy of Errors 3. 2. 96-97

If she lives till doomsday she'll burn a week longer than the whole world.

The Comedy of Errors 3. 2. 97-98

She sweats, a man may go over-shoes in the grime of it.

The Comedy of Errors 3. 2. 101-2

Come, come, you talk greasily; your lips grow foul.

Love's Labour's Lost 4. 1. 136

How shall I be revenged on him? I think the best way were to entertain him with hope till the wicked fire of lust have melted him in his own grease.

The Merry Wives of Windsor 2. 1. 63-66

I think the devil will not have [you] damned, lest the oil that's in [you] should set hell on fire.

The Merry Wives of Windsor 5. 5. 35-36

CATERWAULING

She does abuse to our ears.

All's Well That Ends Well 5. 3. 288

I count it but time lost to hear such a foolish song.

As You Like It 5. 3. 43-44

God mend your voices.

As You Like It 5. 3. 44-45

While she is here, a man may live as quiet in hell as in a sanctuary, and people sin upon purpose, because they would go thither.

Much Ado About Nothing 2. 1. 241-43

Tax not so bad a voice
To slander music any more than once.

Much Ado About Nothing 2. 3. 44-45

If you have any music that may not be heard, to 't again.

Othello 3. 1. 16

I know she is an irksome brawling scold.

The Taming of the Shrew 1. 2. 186

UNWHOLESOME INGESTIONS

DINING

Such boil'd stuff as well might poison poison!

Cymbeline 1. 7. 125-26

Peas and beans are as dank here as a dog, and that is
the best way to give poor jades the bots.

Henry IV, part 1 2. 1. 8-9

Thy food is such
As hath been belch'd on by infected lungs.

Pericles 4. 6. 167-68

IMBIBING

Thou didst drink
The stale of horses, and the gilded puddle
Which beasts would cough at.

Antony and Cleopatra 1. 4. 61-63

I am sure,
Though you know what temperance should be,
You know not what it is.

Antony and Cleopatra 3. 13. 120-22

Drink, Sir, is a great provoker of three things: nose-
painting, sleep, and urine.

Macbeth 2. 3. 26

His days are foul and his drink dangerous.

Timon of Athens 3. 5. 75

BASIC BADNESS

COWARDICE

There's no more valour in [him] than in a wild duck.

Henry IV, part 1   2. 2. 95-96

[You are] essentially a natural coward without instinct.

Henry IV, part 1   2. 4. 486-88

Thou wilt be as valiant as the wrathful dove, or most magnanimous mouse.

Henry IV, part 2   3. 2. 157-58

Thou thing of no bowels thou!

Troilus and Cressida   2. 1. 52

DECEIT

He's a most notable coward, an infinite and endless liar, an hourly promise-breaker, the owner of no one good quality.

All's Well That Ends Well   3. 6. 9-11

Your bait of falsehood takes this carp of truth.

Hamlet   2. 1. 63

I am well acquainted with your manner of wrenching the true cause the false way.

Henry IV, part 2   2. 1. 107-9

This knave's tongue begins to double.

Henry VI, part 2   2. 3. 89

God and good men hate so foul a liar.

Richard II 1. 1. 114

Though [he] is not naturally honest, [he] is so sometimes by chance.

The Winter's Tale 4. 4. 712-13

DISLOYALTY

His kisses are Judas's own children.

As You Like It 3. 4. 7-8

There's no more faith in thee than in a stewed prune.

Henry IV , part 1 3. 3. 110-11

From th' extremist upward of thy head
To the descent and dust below thy foot,
A most toad-spotted traitor.

King Lear 5. 3. 138-40

Thou disease of a friend!

Timon of Athens 3. 1. 53

PRIDE

[You] flatter [yourself] in project of a power
Much smaller than the smallest of [your] thoughts.

Henry IV, part 2 1. 3. 29-30

Your horse would trot as well were some of your brags dismounted.

Henry V 3. 7. 79-80

I can see his pride peep through each part of him.

Henry VIII 1. 1. 68-69

SLOTH

Every day that comes comes to decay a day's work in him.

Cymbeline 1. 6. 56-57

I abhor this dilatory sloth.

Henry VIII 2. 4. 234-35

BOTCHERS AND LIGHTWEIGHTS

WANT-WITS

How prove you that in the great heap of your knowledge?

As You Like It 1. 2. 66-67

His brain is as dry as the remainder biscuit after a voyage.

As You Like It 2. 7. 38-40

[He] in gross brain little wots.

Henry V 4. 1. 288

Your mind is tossing on the ocean.

The Merchant of Venice 1. 1. 8

Thou wilt fall backward when thou hast more wit.

Romeo and Juliet 1. 3. 42

There will little learning die then that day thou art hang'd.

Timon of Athens 2. 2. 85-86

[You're] a fusty nut with no kernel.

Troilus and Cressida 2. 1. 103-4

Would the fountain of your mind were clear again, that I might water an ass at it.

Troilus and Cressida 3. 3. 308-9

He has not so much brain as ear-wax.

Troilus and Cressida 5. 1. 51-52

SHORT-FALLING AND OVER-REACHING

You go so much backward when you fight.

All's Well That Ends Well 1. 1. 196

In his sleep he does little harm, save to his bedclothes about him.

All's Well That Ends Well 4. 3. 246-48

Thou art so leaky
That we must leave thee to thy sinking.

Antony and Cleopatra 3. 13. 63-64

His passions, like a whale on ground,
Confound themselves with working.

Henry IV, part 2 4. 4. 40-41

No man's pie is freed from [your] ambitious finger.

Henry VIII 1. 1. 53

UNDERHANDING

Be better employed, and be naught awhile.

As You Like It 1. 1. 34-35

[You] confirmer of false reckonings.

As You Like It 3. 4. 30

A brace of unmeriting, proud, violent, testy magistrates (alias fools).

Coriolanus 2. 1. 43-45

> I am whipp'd and scourg'd with rods,
> Nettled, and stung with pismires, when I hear
> Of this vile politician.

Henry IV, part 1 1. 3. 236-38

They will steal any thing and call it purchase.

Henry V 3. 2. 44

Get thee glass eyes; and, like a scurvy politician, seem to see the things thou dost not.

King Lear 4. 6. 172-74

What's here? the portrait of a blinking idiot, Presenting me a schedule!

Merchant of Venice 2. 9. 54-55

I will knog your urinal about your knave's cogscomb for missing your meetings and appointments.

The Merry Wives of Windsor 3. 3. 81-82

You are thought here to be the most senseless and fit man for the [job].

Much Ado About Nothing 3. 3. 22-23

BOORS AND BORES

THE CONTEMPTIBLE

Methink'st thou art a general offence and every man should beat thee.

All's Well That Ends Well 2. 3. 250-51

I think thou wast created for men to breathe themselves upon thee.

All's Well That Ends Well 2. 3. 251-52

It is a deadly sorrow to behold a foul knave uncuckolded.

Antony and Cleopatra 1. 2. 69-70

Sell when you can, you are not for all markets.

As You Like It 3. 5. 60

Take a good heart, and counterfeit to be a man.

As You Like It 4. 3. 173-74

What a disgrace is it to me to remember thy name.

Henry IV , part 2 2. 2. 12-13

To die by thee were but to die in jest.

Henry VI, part 2 3. 2. 399

All that is within him does condemn itself for being there.

Macbeth 5. 2. 24-25

Canst thou believe thy living is a life,
So stinkingly depending? Go mend, go mend.

Measure for Measure 3. 2. 25-26

It appears by his small light of discretion that he is in the wane.

A Midsummer Night's Dream   5. 1. 243-44

[You are] duller than a great thaw.

Much Ado About Nothing   2. 1. 228

Were I like thee I'd throw away myself.

Timon of Athens   4. 3. 221

Would thou wert clean enough to spit upon!

Timon of Athens   4. 3. 361

What folly I commit, I dedicate to you.

Troilus and Cressida 3. 2. 101-2

THE INSIGNIFICANT

So, my good window of lattice, fare thee well; thy casement I need not open, for I look through thee.

All's Well That Ends Well   2. 3. 213-14

There can be no kernel in this light nut; the soul of this man is his clothes.

All's Well That Ends Well   2. 5. 42-44

We do bear so great weight in his lightness.

Antony and Cleopatra 1. 4. 25

Is his head worth a hat? Or his chin worth a beard?

As You Like It 3. 2. 202-3

When the sun shines let foolish gnats make sport.

The Comedy of Errors 2. 2. 30

[You are] such toasts-and-butter, with hearts in [your] bellies no bigger than pins' heads!

Henry IV, part 1 4. 2. 20-22

You are the fount that makes small brooks to flow.

Henry VI, part 3 4. 8. 54

You are not worth the dust which the rude wind blows in your face.

King Lear 4. 2. 30-31

Vile worm, thou wast o'erlook'd even in thy birth.

The Merry Wives of Windsor 5. 5. 84

[You] small grey-coated gnat.

Romeo and Juliet 1. 4. 67

[You are] a slave whose gall coins slanders like a mint!

Troilus and Cressida 1. 3. 193

[You] whose grossness little characters sum up!

Troilus and Cressida 1. 3. 324-25

THE UNDESIREABLE

What poor an instrument.

Antony and Cleopatra 5. 2. 235

I had as lief be wooed of a snail.

As You Like It 4. 1. 49

She should have me as a beast: not that, I being a beast she would have me; but that she, being a very beastly creature, lays claim to me.

Comedy of Errors 3. 2. 94-95

I have but lean luck in the match, and yet is she a wondrous fat marriage.

Comedy of Errors 3. 2. 100-1

As from a bear a man would run for life,
So fly I from her that would be my wife.

Comedy of Errors 3. 2. 164-65

[You are] the bluntest wooer in Christendom.

Henry VI, part 3 3. 2. 83

I had rather be married to a death's-head with a bone in
his mouth.

The Merchant of Venice 1. 2. 49-50

I will do any thing ere I will be married to a sponge.

The Merchant of Venice 1. 2. 94-95

[I won't be fitted with a husband], not till God make men
of some other metal than earth. Would it not grieve a
woman to be over-mastered with a piece of valiant dust,
to make an account of her life to a clod of wayward marl?

Much Ado About Nothing 2. 1. 55-58

I do care for something; but in my conscience, sir, I do
not care for you: if that be to care for nothing, sir, I would
it would make you invisible.

Twelfth Night 3. 1. 28-31

LOOSENESS AND TIGHTNESS

LASCIVIOUSNESS

I knew [him to] be a dangerous and lascivious boy, who is

a whale to virginity, and devours up all the fry it finds.

All's Well That Ends Well 4. 3. 212-13

She was a common gamester to the camp.

All's Well That Ends Well 5. 3. 187

He fill'd his vacancy with his voluptuousness.

Antony and Cleopatra 1. 4. 25-26

Tie up the libertine in a field of feasts.

Antony and Cleopatra 1. 5. 23

[You are] one that converses more with the buttock of the night than with the forehead of the morning.

Coriolanus 2. 11. 50-52

[You are] an index and prologue to the history of lust and foul thoughts.

Othello 2. 1. 254-55

[He] wears his wit in his belly and his guts in his head.

Troilus and Cressida 2. 1. 75-76

STODGINESS

Your virginity, your old virginity, is like one of our French wither'd pears: it looks ill, it eats drily.

All's Well That Ends Well 1. 1. 156-57

He hath bought a pair of cast lips of Diana. A nun of winter's sisterhood kisses not more religiously, the very ice of chastity is in them.

As You Like It 3. 4. 14-16

I never knew so young a body with so old a head.
The Merchant of Venice 4. 1. 160-61

[You] stale old mouse-eaten dry cheese!
Troilus and Cressida 5. 4. 10-11

WINDBAGGERY

Thus he his special nothing ever prologues.
All's Well That Ends Well 2. 1. 91

Much fool may you find in you, even to the world's pleasure and the increase of laughter.
All's Well That Ends Well 2. 4. 34-35

I find the ass in compound with the major part of your syllables.
Coriolanus 2. 1. 57-58

All the peace you make in their cause is calling both the parties knaves.
Coriolanus 2. 1. 77-79

More of your conversation would infect my brain.
Coriolanus 2. 1. 93-94

Why should she live to fill the world with words?
Henry VI, part 3 5. 5. 43

He draweth out the thread of his verbosity finer than the staple of his argument.
Love's Labour's Lost 5. 1. 17-18

They have been at a great feast of languages, and stolen the scraps.

Love's Labour's Lost   5. 1. 37-38

[You] speak an infinite deal of nothing.

The Merchant of Venice   1. 1. 113

Wilt thou show the whole wealth of thy wit in an instant?

The Merchant of Venice 3. 5. 50-51

How fiery and forward our pedant is!

The Taming of the Shrew 3. 1. 46

      [Thy] learned pate
Ducks to the golden fool.

Timon of Athens 4. 3. 17-18

INDEX

Note: Insults are indexed by number; **boldface** figures refer to pages.

villains (*cont.*)
  minds of, 3027
  naked, 3454
  name-calling, **16–18,** 2101,
    2239–40, 2776, 3277, 4084
  paper-faced, 2390
  poison for, 1795
  as ubiquitous, 2174
  vile deeds of, 1819, 2145,
    2437, 2783, 3206, 3266
  vile stuff for, 2889, 3126
  see also knaves
virginity, 1752–54, 3371
  casting away of, 1758
  excessive, 1926, 3387
  as recommended, 2132
  threats to, *see* lasciviousness
virtue:
  easy, 1832, 1835–36, 2058,
    2153, 2867, 3383, 3848,
    3890–91, 3910, 4139
  of little regard, 2277
vultures, 2131, 2388, 2411,
    3066, 3588, 4153

W
want-wits, **299–300,** 1891, 2109,
    2339, 2357, 2365, 2462,
    3009–10, 3106, 3193,
    3230, 3238, 3259, 3295,
    3305, 3517, 3563, 3640,
    3724, 3857, 3881, 3883
  age and, 3795
  animals compared with,
    2522, 3172, 3453
  beauty and, 2051–53
  blockheads, 2020
  brains and, 1905, 2093, 2171,
    2221, 2476, 2510, 2903,
    2934, 3111, 3335, 3670,
    3847, 3852, 3941
  empty heads of, 2459, 2974,
    3491, 3855
  fatheads, 2913

fools and, 1890, 2093, 3729
  inadequacy of, 2903, 2911,
    3044, 3171, 3959
  meat-eaters, 3926
  out of repair, 3051
  overuse of, 2860, 4046
  politicians, 3670
  repetition by, 2914
  short-lived, 2859
  spouses, 2713
  stale, 3522
  tainted, 3995
  and weak body, 2120
waspishness, 2746, 3589
wastefulness, 2275, 3285
weapons, 3486, 3799–800
  eyes as, 2546, 2579
  for madmen, 2578
  in speech, 2862
  words as, 2091, 2154, 3211
whoremasters, 3724–25
wickedness, 2553, 2797,
    2947–48, 3633
  audacious, 2526
  facinerious, 1769
  heinous, 3420
  lascivious, 2556
  malignant, 2671
  pernicious, 3346
  of relatives, 3694
  and sin, 2332, 2375, 2957,
    2984
  tainted, 1792
windbaggery, **307–8,** 2010,
    2014, 2098, 2444, 2648,
    2862, 2892, 3886
  animals and, 2006, 3363
  bombastic, 2234, 2324
    2762, 2772–74
  empty, 1764, 2179, 2485,
    2964, 3015, 3507, 3647,
    3880
  fools and, 1786, 3751
  fragmented, 3190